Ben Franklin's
PHILADELPHIA

A Guide

TOM HUNTINGTON

STACKPOLE BOOKS

917.48
HUN

Published by
STACKPOLE BOOKS
5067 Ritter Road
Mechanicsburg, PA 17055
www.stackpolebooks.com

Printed in the United States of America

10 9 8 7 6 5 4 3 2 1

FIRST EDITION

Design by Beth Oberholtzer
Cover design by Caroline Stover

Photographs by the author unless otherwise noted

Cover: *Ralph Archbold as Benjamin Franklin*
PHOTO BY ALAN WYCHECK

Library of Congress Cataloging-in-Publication Data

Huntington, Tom.
    Ben Franklin's Philadelphia : a guide / Tom Huntington.— 1st ed.
        p.   cm.
    Includes bibliographical references and index.
    ISBN-13: 978-0-8117-3282-6 (pbk.)
    ISBN-10: 0-8117-3282-7 (pbk.)
    1. Philadelphia (Pa.)—Tours. 2. Franklin, Benjamin, 1706-1790
—Homes and haunts—Pennsylvania—Philadelphia—Guidebooks.
3. Philadelphia (Pa.)—History—Colonial period, ca. 1600–1775—Biography. 4. Philadelphia (Pa.)—History—Revolution, 1775–1783—Biography. 5. Historic buildings—Pennsylvania—Philadelphia—Guidebooks.
6. Franklin, Benjamin, 1706–1790—Friends and associates. I. Title.

F158.18.H86   2006
917.48'11—dc22

                                                    2005024730

Contents

★

Site Directory

★

Preface

★

Benjamin Franklin once observed some flies that had apparently drowned in Madeira but began moving again after some time in the sun. It started him thinking, as such things often did. "Having a very ardent desire to see and observe the state of America a hundred years hence, I should prefer to any ordinary death the being immersed in a cask of Madeira wine, with a few friends, till that time, to be then recalled to life by the solar warmth of my dear country," he wrote.

If such things were possible, who would derive the greater pleasure — Franklin or us? I have no doubt Franklin would be delighted by wonders of electricity, the progress of science, and the fabulous growth of the nation he helped create. No doubt he would initially be taken aback by the sights of modern Philadelphia — the skyscrapers in Central City, the roaring buses, the huge jets flying overhead to and from the airport. But I think that after his initial shock and disbelief, Franklin would take it all in stride, even at the ripe old age of three hundred.

For our part, we could enjoy Franklin's company. Of all the founding fathers, Franklin seems to have been the most approachable. He was noted for his wit and warmth, whereas George Washington was aloof and untouchable, Jefferson somewhat shy and slippery, John Adams paranoid and cranky. Franklin, on the other hand, was someone who could make people laugh, tell them something interesting, and help them look at things in new ways. Although he was born three centuries ago, Franklin still seems like a contemporary, someone it would be fun to spend time with.

Franklin isn't likely to be emerging from a cask of Madeira anytime soon, so we'll have to make do with what we have. Philadelphia, the city that Franklin made his home, will be celebrating his tercentenary throughout 2006. It's the perfect time to visit the city and find traces of its most famous citizen. This guide is an attempt to help you in your search. It's not meant to be a biography; you can find plenty of those at the library or bookstore. Instead, it seeks out the things Franklin left behind in his adopted home — even though he spent so much of his life away from it. Consider it a literary version of one of Franklin's innovations, the bifocals, something to help you shift your focus between past and present.

Born in Boston in 1706, Franklin reached Philadelphia at the age of seventeen, when both he and the city were young but filled with promise. Much has changed over the centuries, and much has been lost forever. Busy, growing cities like Philadelphia don't always take time to look back. In 1812, Franklin's relatives tore down his house and the valuable land was subdivided. In 1816, the state legislature even proposed razing the old State House, the very building that had seen the birth of the Declaration of Independence and the U.S. Constitution, but fortunately that didn't happen.

Yes, much has changed in Philadelphia since Franklin's day, but enough remains to stir the imagination. People at the various sites, such as Franklin interpreters Dean Bennett and Ralph Archbold, National Park Service rangers, and curators and historians, can help you use what's left to turn on the time machine inside your head and return to the era when Benjamin Franklin walked the streets of Philadelphia.

Many people were generous with their time and knowledge to help me with this guide. Those who shared their enthusiasm about Franklin and Philadelphia included Roy E. Goodman of the American Philosophical Society; James Green of the Library

Company of Philadelphia; Anna Coxe Toogood, historian at Independence National Historical Park; John Alviti and Stacey Persichetti at the Franklin Institute; Del Conner at the Philadelphia Society for the Preservation of Landmarks; Robert Vosburgh at Elfreth's Alley; and Neil Ronk at Christ Church. Dean Bennett and Ralph Archbold made me feel as though I had actually met Franklin—twice! In addition, I offer a heartfelt thank-you to all the guides and park rangers who provided answers to my questions at the various sites.

Thanks to Dr. George Boudreau, Assistant Professor of American Studies and History at Penn State Harrisburg, for reading the manuscript and pointing out where I wandered off the path of historical accuracy. Any errors that remain, of course, are mine and mine alone.

Donna Schorr of the Greater Philadelphia Tourism Marketing Corporation was kind enough to arrange accommodations for me in Philadelphia, and I'd like to thank the staffs at the Penn's View and Radisson Plaza–Warwick Hotels for making my stays there so enjoyable. GPTMC's Cara Schneider provided valuable advice and support.

Thanks also to Kyle Weaver, my editor at Stackpole Books, who came up with the idea for this book and asked me to write it. I appreciate your confidence in me.

This guidebook could not have happened without the love and support of my wife, Beth Ann, who has faith in me even when I don't. Baby, you're the best. And my children, Katie and Sam, made exploring Franklin's Philadelphia even more fun than it would have been otherwise.

Dean Bennett as Franklin

Beginnings

"Enjoy a taste of history!" reads the chalkboard on the sidewalk outside Philadelphia's City Tavern, a reconstruction of the inn John Adams called "the most genteel in America." My waiter refers to it as a "culinary museum." Chef Walter Staib uses period recipes and ingredients; the goblets, plates, and cutlery are pewter; and the servers wear eighteenth-century costumes. I even spot a harpsichord in the front room.

The original City Tavern opened in 1773 and was demolished following a fire in 1854. The National Park Service built this one in 1975, just in time for the nation's bicentennial. It's perfectly appropriate, then, to dine in this re-created inn with a re-created Benjamin Franklin.

Dean Bennett has been performing as Franklin since 1981, taking the role for the first time right here in the courtyard behind City Tavern. He has appeared at the White House and the National Archives in Washington, D.C., in Las Vegas, and even in France, when an airline flew him and a Thomas Jefferson impersonator to Paris for inauguration of service there. With his wig, glasses, gold-topped cane, frock coat, and vest, he bears a striking resemblance to our most lovable founding father. "He's like everybody's favorite uncle," says Bennett, who tells me the role has been an educational experience. "Here in Philadelphia, everyone knows something about Ben Franklin, so they'd come up and check to see if you knew what you were supposed to know. I found that I couldn't bluff it—I didn't want to bluff it—so ultimately I went ahead and got some books, and now I can talk for quite a length about Franklin."

One topic people often raise is Franklin's reputation with women, especially his relationships while serving as American commissioner to France from 1776 to 1785. "That is a very hot topic, the ladies of France," Bennett says, though he thinks it's a shame that Franklin has earned a reputation as America's founding rake. "Actually, when he went over there, he was seventy years old, he had gout, he had stones of the bladder, and he had shingles. So he was not in the very best of health." Furthermore, Bennett adds, Franklin's wife had died in 1774. "It wasn't like he was sneaking off trying to have a fling with some young chick. I always explain that they should keep in mind that he was sent there by Congress, so anything he did with those ladies he did as a patriot."

City Tavern

138 S. Second St. ★ (215) 413-1443
www.citytavern.com

It may not be the original, but this reproduction City Tavern will give you a good taste of eighteenth-century dining. In its day, City Tavern was "in the latest London mode"; the appeal of the current version is that there's nothing of the latest mode about it at all. Some of its specialties include West Indies pepperpot soup and a chocolate mousse made from Martha Washington's recipe. It also serves beer made from recipes handed down from George Washington and Thomas Jefferson. City Tavern is open for lunch and dinner daily. Reservations are recommended.

City Tavern

Yet Franklin was a man who savored what life offered him. It would not have been unusual to find him at an inn like the City Tavern, for he enjoyed eating and drinking. His claim to have been "bro't up in such a perfect Inattention to these matters as to be quite Indifferent what kind of Food was set before me" wasn't necessarily true. In France, he left behind a wine cellar with twelve hundred bottles. He composed drinking songs. While in England, Franklin wrote to a friend, the botanist John Bartram, that he would prefer a traveler to Italy send him a recipe for Parmesan cheese rather than translations of ancient inscriptions.

For a man who enjoyed wine and song (and, yes, women), Philadelphia was a good place to live. Its Quaker founders disapproved of taverns, but they couldn't prevent them. By 1750, Philadelphia had 120 drinking establishments. "There was a public house to suit every purse and every taste, from innumerable sailors' groggeries down by the wharves to Daniel Smith's famous City Tavern," note Carl and Jessica Bridenbaugh in *Rebels and Gentlemen: Philadelphia in the Age of Franklin.*

Bennett has arrived at City Tavern on this day dressed as Franklin, and visitors do double takes as they enter the dining room and see that the lunch specials include a Founding Father. They shouldn't be too surprised, though, because Franklin is a familiar sight in today's Philadelphia. Founder William Penn has a higher perch atop City Hall, but Franklin has superiority in numbers. Far below Penn's gaze at Broad Street and John F. Kennedy Boulevard, Franklin the printer works his press in a statue by Joseph Brown. Another sculpted Franklin lounges on a park bench reading a newspaper at the University of Pennsylvania, an institution he helped found. A thirty-ton, twenty-foot-tall Franklin dominates the rotunda at the Franklin Institute.

Franklin is a staple in the local gift shops. At the Franklin Institute, you can buy a Ben Franklin action figure, complete with tiny kite. The National Constitution Center offers a Franklin bobblehead. The store at the Lights of Liberty sound-and-vision show sells all kinds of Ben Franklin ware, from cookie jars to shot glasses.

Elsewhere in the old city, you can shop at Ben's Shoes or buy an ice cream at Franklin's Fountain. Near Independence Hall on Chestnut Street, a cartoon Franklin scampers across the sign for Benny's Place. Franklin peers from the logo for a concert venue called the Electric Factory,

Benny's Place and Ben's Shoes

and he wears leiderhosen and brandishes a beer stein in ads for the Independence Brew House. You can visit Franklin Square, cross the Benjamin Franklin Bridge, or drive down the Benjamin Franklin Parkway.

The funny thing is, Franklin wasn't even from here. He was born in humble surroundings in Boston on January 6, 1706. (The date was changed to January 17 when the calendar was adjusted in 1752.) His father, Josiah, had arrived in Massachusetts from England in 1683, shortly after William Penn received a royal charter for an American colony called Pennsylvania. Josiah had seventeen children by his two wives. Benjamin's mother, Abiah, was Josiah's second wife, and Franklin was his fifteenth child and youngest son. As Franklin learned when he visited England, he was "the youngest Son of the youngest Son for 5 Generations back."

In Boston, Josiah began making candles and soap for a living. He took Ben out of school at age ten to help him make candles, an occupation the boy disliked. Worried that his headstrong youngest son might run away to sea, Josiah decided to apprentice him to his son James, a printer.

Ben was already demonstrating the active, questing intelligence that would characterize him throughout his life. When he found bound copies of the English literary magazine the *Spectator* in his brother's shop, he used them to polish his own writing. He rewrote the essays, cutting them apart and putting them back together again. He practiced turning prose into verse, and then back into prose. "Then I compar'd my Spectator with the Original," he wrote years later. "I discover'd many faults and amended them; but I sometimes had the Pleasure of Fancying that in certain Particulars of small Import, I had been lucky enough to improve the Method or the Language and this encourag'd me to think I might possibly in time come to be a tolerable English Writer, of which I was extreamely ambitious."

Working for his brother gave Ben an opportunity for literary fame, albeit under another name. At the time, James printed the *New England Courant*, one of the colonies' first papers. Ben doubted his older brother would let him write for the paper, so he signed his writings "Silence Dogood" and slipped them under James's door. He wrote the pieces in the voice of a tart-tongued New England woman and was delighted to listen as James and his friends speculated about the author's true identity.

Ben enjoyed the work of printing but chafed under his older brother's tutelage. "I fancy his harsh and tyrannical Treatment of me, might be a means of impressing me with that Aversion to arbitrary Power that has stuck to me thro' my whole life," he noted in his autobiography. Then again, he admitted, perhaps he was "too saucy and provoking."

Whether he was saucy or oppressed—probably a little of both—by 1723, Franklin had had enough. He sold some of his books, booked passage on a ship under the guise that he "had got a naughty Girl with Child," and ran away from Boston four years before his apprenticeship was over. Three days later, he was in New York City, "a Boy of but 17, without the least Recommendation to or Knowledge of any Person in the Place, and with very little Money in my Pocket."

In New York, Franklin introduced himself to William Bradford. Bradford had been Philadelphia's first printer, but he decamped for New York after clashing with local authorities. He had no work for Franklin, Bradford said, but his son Andrew was still in Philadelphia and had a vacancy. Franklin headed for Philadelphia.

William Penn's City of Brotherly Love was scarcely older than Franklin. Penn, the son of a prominent English admiral of the same name, had appeared destined to join the British establishment. Instead, in 1667, he converted to the Society of Friends, a religious group George Fox had founded fifteen years earlier. The Quakers, as they became known, believed that God spoke directly to everyone—Christians and non-Christians alike—eliminating the need for priests or an organized church structure. The establishment didn't like that much and tried to quash the Quakers. Penn himself spent time in prison for his beliefs. In 1681, as payment for a debt owed to Penn's father, and perhaps just to get Penn and his ilk out of his hair, King Charles II gave young William the land in North America that became known as Pennsylvania (after the admiral, not the son). Penn picked a site

Gloria Dei (Old Swedej') Church

916 Swanson St. ★ (215) 389-1513
www.nps.gov/glde
or www.old-swedes.org

Dating to 1700, Gloria Dei is a reminder that the Swedish settled here before the English. Originally a Lutheran Church, it became Episcopalian in 1845. It is a little off the beaten path, but well worth a visit. Gloria Dei is a working church as well as a national historic site. It's probably a good idea to call ahead before visiting to make sure it's open.

between the Delaware and Schuylkill Rivers as the spot for a future metropolis he named Philadelphia, after a city in the Bible. The name, loosely translated, means City of Brotherly Love.

The area's first European colonists had been Swedes, who arrived in 1643. The Dutch replaced the Swedes, and England later claimed the region in 1664, but you can find a reminder of the Swedish presence at the Gloria Dei Church, popularly known as Old Swedes'. The church building was dedicated in 1700 and today stands in a somewhat industrialized neighborhood among overpasses and I-95 south of the old city. There's nothing about the building that screams "Sweden." It's a neat, little brick church surrounded by a small cemetery and compact gardens. Suspended from the ceiling inside are models of the *Kalmar Nyckel* and *Fogel Grip*, two ships that brought Swedes to the New World in 1643. Betsy Ross of flag fame married her second husband, Joseph Ashburn, at this church in 1777.

The church lay outside the boundaries of the town Penn laid out. Using "the latest in urban planning," he gave his city a grid pattern, with eight streets running east to west from the Delaware to the Schuylkill and named after "things that Spontaneously grow in the Country"—hence the city's Vine Street, Chestnut Street, Walnut Street, and Mulberry Street (later changed to Arch). Penn numbered the north-south streets, with the exception of Broad Street. He urged his colonists to build in the center of their lots, leaving plenty of space on all sides to provide safety from fires.

The city grew slowly and in a less orderly fashion than Penn had hoped. When Franklin reached Philadelphia in 1723, there were no paved streets, and the population was only about five thousand. Until 1731, hogs were allowed to run loose, provided they bore the owner's brand.

It was in this small but growing town, still virtually a frontier community compared with Boston, that Franklin arrived one Sunday morning in October 1723. He disembarked on the city's Market Street Wharf from a boat that had brought him down the Delaware River from New Jersey. "I was in my working Dress,

Penn's Landing
www.pennslandingcorp.com

Franklin first set foot in Philadelphia at Market Street Wharf in 1723. Today the site is part of Penn's Landing, so named because William Penn came ashore here when he arrived in Pennsylvania in 1682. Running along the Delaware River waterfront from Market Street to Lombard Street, Penn's Landing provides a fine place to walk and enjoy views of the river and the 1,750-foot-long Benjamin Franklin Bridge. You can also visit the Independence Seaport Museum and see the *Olympia*, Commodore George Dewey's flagship at the 1898 Battle of Manila Bay, and the World War II submarine *Becuna*. The huge gray warship on the opposite shore is the battleship *New Jersey*, open to the public in Camden, New Jersey. Ferries at Penn's Landing will take you over. Look down the river to spot the smokestacks of the SS *United States*, once the fastest liner on the seas and now a rusting, stripped-down hulk. In 1952, she crossed the Atlantic in three days, ten hours, and forty-two minutes. It took Franklin more than six weeks to travel from England to Philadelphia in 1775.

Penn's Landing

my best Cloaths being to come round by Sea," he wrote in his autobiography. "I was dirty from my Journey; my Pockets were stuff'd out with Shirts and Stockings; I knew no Soul, nor where to look for Lodging. I was fatigu'd with Travelling, Rowing and Want of Rest. I was very hungry, and my whole Stock of Cash consisted of a Dutch Dollar and about a Shilling in Copper."

Franklin found a bakery and purchased three large rolls for three pennies, then began exploring. "Thus I went up Market-street as far as fourth Street, passing by the Door of Mr. Read, my future Wife's Father; when she, standing at the Door, saw me, and thought I made as I certainly did, a most awkward, ridiculous Appearance." Franklin may have been a little self-deprecating when he wrote that, for it's equally likely young Deborah Read noticed something cocky and self-confident about this young man with his rolls. Benjamin Franklin never lacked self-confidence. He had already made something of a name for himself in Boston. No doubt he felt that Philadelphia could be his for the taking.

"Then I turn'd and went down Chestnut-street and part of Walnut-street, eating my Roll all the Way, and, coming round, found myself again at Market Street Wharff, near the Boat I came in, to which I went for a Draught of the River Water; and,

Elfreth's Alley

being fill'd with one of my Rolls, gave the other two to a Woman
and her Child that came down the River in the Boat with us, and
were waiting to go farther."

A visitor to Franklin's Philadelphia would be advised to take
a page from Ben's book and wander a bit. The city is now a
sprawling megalopolis with a population of about 1.5 million, so
it does take a prodigious exercise of the imagination to see the
city as Franklin first saw it. The wharf where he came ashore is
now called Penn's Landing, and it hardly resembles the busy
commercial waterfront that existed then. In fact, it's difficult to
find much of anything remaining from 1723 Philadelphia.

You can catch a fleeting glimpse of early Philadelphia at
Elfreth's Alley, a narrow lane off Second Street north of Arch.
This national historic landmark claims to be "Our Nation's Oldest Street," and its upstanding brick buildings, brick sidewalks,
and cobblestones do make it seem as out of time as a quill pen or
powdered wig. The alley dates back to around 1702, when it was
a route used by workers taking their carts to and from the

bustling waterfront. "We're pretty certain that by 1713 there were houses on the block, none of which have survived," says Robert Vosburgh, director of the Elfreth's Alley Museum. "How many homes were here by 1723 is tough to say." The oldest remaining buildings date from the later 1720s. Blacksmith Jeremiah Elfreth built some homes here in the 1750s and gave the alley its name. Two of his later buildings, numbers 124 and 126, operate today as a small museum. In 1762, sisters-in-law Mary Smith and Sarah Milton bought number 126 from Elfreth and worked here making fancy cloaks called mantuas. Smith and Milton were examples of the alley's "middling" class of artisans and tradespeople in the 1700s. So was John Ackley, who sometime in the later 1700s began making Windsor chairs and possibly sold them from his home at number 124.

Over the years, the alley's fortunes ebbed and flowed. Starting in 1934, the nonprofit Elfreth's Alley Association worked to save the alley from demolition. One of the founders, Dolly Ottey,

Elfreth's Alley

124–126 Elfreth's Alley ★ (215) 574-0560

www.elfrethsalley.org

Elfreth's Alley is the oldest continually occupied residential street in America. Although there is no evidence that Franklin visited here, he probably passed by. Two of the alley's buildings, numbers 124 and 126, house the Elfreth's Alley Museum. Hours from March through October are Monday through Saturday from 10 A.M. to 5 P.M. and Sunday from noon to 5 P.M. The rest of the year, it's open Thursday through Saturday from 10 A.M. to 5 P.M. and Sunday from noon to 5 P.M. Admission is $3 for adults and $1 for children ages six to eighteen. Deck the Alley, a candlelit celebration of the holidays, takes place in December; the Fete Days festival is held in June. People still live in the homes here, and they ask that you respect their privacy.

operated a tearoom called the Hearthstone in number 115, where you could buy chipped beef on toast for 15 cents and maybe learn a little bit about the alley's history. In the 1950s, planners wanted to smash Interstate 95 right through the alley, but the association fought to save the street and won it designation as a national historic landmark. In the years since, it has become an increasingly popular tourist attraction. The museum opened in the early 1960s, and now a quarter million people wander through the alley each year or come for its two annual events, the candlelit Deck the Alley evenings in December and Fete Days in June.

Elfreth's Alley is more than a museum piece, though. People still live here, an unbroken chain of life that has lasted for almost three centuries. It's certainly cleaner and neater than it was in the eighteenth century, according to Vosburgh, and while tourists may marvel at its quaintness, Elfreth's Alley is still the real thing. "This is a place where people lived, and live," he says.

Vosburgh tells me that on nearby Water Street I can find one remaining artifact from the time of Franklin's arrival: a small

Atwater Kent Museum of Philadelphia

15 S. Seventh St. ★ (215) 685-4830
www.philadelphiahistory.org

Those interested in a broader overview of Philadelphia's past should visit the Atwater Kent Museum. The city's official history museum, it opened in 1941 in the Franklin Institute's original home. The museum's benefactor, A. Atwater Kent, was an inventor whose beautiful radios are much prized by collectors today. The museum's central exhibit, "Experience Philadelphia!" includes a forty-by-forty-foot map that you can walk across. The museum is open Wednesday through Sunday from 1 to 5 P.M. Admission is $5 for adults and $3 for seniors and teens between thirteen and seventeen. Kids twelve and under are free.

flight of stone stairs dating to around 1719. Finding the stairway isn't easy, though, as it has no plaques or markers, and even the street is not on any of my maps. Water Street used to be a main road along the Delaware, but wider, traffic-friendly routes have swallowed it up, and only a tiny portion remains.

After wandering along some decrepit cobblestoned streets just north of the Benjamin Franklin Bridge, I finally spot a sad, little sign for Water Street. It is little more than an alley running through a neighborhood that appears poised on the brink of gentrification, between I-95 and busy Christopher Columbus Boulevard. Finally, I find a simple set of granite stairs leading down between two modern residential buildings toward the river. As rough and mundane as they appear, they are a direct link to Franklin's era, mute witnesses to almost three hundred years of Philadelphia history.

Maybe Franklin used these steps during his initial stay in Philadelphia, but he wasn't here long. He took lodgings in the Market Street house of John Read, whose daughter Deborah had observed Franklin with such amusement. He and Deborah began a courtship of sorts. Bradford's job lead didn't pan out, but the Bradfords helped him get work at the printing house of Samuel Keimer, an eccentric man with odd religious enthusiasms, a huge beard, and an uncertain grasp of his trade. Franklin helped put his business in order, to the older man's increasing resentment. The bright young man also attracted the attention of Gov. Sir William Keith, who took him under his wing and promised to set Franklin up in his own business. Better yet, he suggested that Franklin travel to London and pick out his printing equipment personally. Accordingly, on November 5, 1724, Benjamin Franklin left Philadelphia for his first visit to England.

The opportunity must have seemed too good to be true—and it was. Sir William, Franklin learned, was much better at making promises than keeping them. When Franklin reached England, he discovered that the governor had not provided the letter of credit he had promised, nor any letters of introduction. Sir William had left Franklin high and dry, a stranger in a strange land, an entire ocean away from his newly adopted home.

The earliest known portrait of
Benjamin Franklin, 1740s, by Robert Feke.

Model Citizen

Despite his initial situation, Franklin did well in London. He found work as a printer, although his fellow workers thought he was odd because he drank water instead of beer and was strong enough to carry two loads of type up the stairs while the others could carry only one. He could have stayed in London, but after about a year and a half, as he wrote, "[I] remember'd with Pleasure the happy Months I had spent in Pennsylvania, and wish'd again to see it." In July 1726, he set sail for home.

Shortly after his return, Franklin encountered the now former governor Keith in the street. Sir William "seem'd a little asham'd at seeing me," he noted. We can only speculate on Deborah Read's feelings. Franklin had sent her only one letter during his eighteen months away, and she had wed a man who may have already been married. He departed for the Caribbean, where he supposedly died. No one knew for sure.

Eventually Franklin ended up back with Keimer. The relationship remained strained, and Franklin finally broke off to start his own printing business, called the New Printing-Office, with another employee of Keimer's, Hugh Meredith. It was initially at 139 Market Street, but in 1739, he moved his home and business to 131 Market Street.

As an ambitious tradesman, Franklin was acutely aware of his public image. He bought his paper supplies himself so that potential customers could see him bumping through the streets with his wheelbarrow, the perfect image of a frugal, hardworking printer. Not that Franklin was perfect. He sowed his wild oats among what he referred to as the "low Women that fell in my Way." He was thankful to have escaped a "Distemper" as a result of these encounters, but he did not escape the other natural result—a child. Around 1731, Franklin had a son, William, by a woman whose identity remains unknown. By then he had taken Deborah Read as his common-law wife. They would remain married until Deborah's death in 1774, and it appears to have been a marriage of affection, if not passion. They had a son, Francis, who died of smallpox at four, and a daughter, Sarah, called Sally.

In 1727, Franklin formed the Junto, "a Club for mutual Improvement" for like-minded, ambitious young men. Members included a copier of deeds, a surveyor, a shoemaker-turned-

Printing Office
320 Market St. ★ (800) 537-7676

The Printing Office is part of Franklin Court, which itself is a portion of Independence National Historical Park. National park rangers perform printing demonstrations here throughout the day. The Printing Office is in 320 Market Street, a building that Franklin never actually owned. Enter from the door inside Franklin Court. The building next door, at number 322, which you can enter directly from the Printing Office, includes the restored office of Benjamin Franklin Bache's *Aurora* newspaper and a book bindery. The Printing Office is usually open from 10 A.M. to 5 P.M., but its hours vary seasonally, so it's a good idea to check in advance. There is no admission charge.

mathematician, a joiner, and a clerk. Franklin's printing partner, Hugh Meredith, and friends Stephen Potts and George Webb also joined, as did Robert Grace, "a young Gentlemen of some Fortune." Another member was William Maugridge, a carpenter and ship joiner related by marriage to Daniel Boone. He lived at number 122 on Elfreth's Alley, so perhaps Franklin visited him there. The Junto met in a room at Grace's house, entering through Pewter Platter Alley. Today this is Church Street, a narrow lane between Second and Front Streets near Christ Church. The members met each Friday night, presenting papers and discussing the questions of the day, with appropriate pauses for wine and socializing. The Junto was like today's service clubs, an organization whose members could help the community and each other. For example, Grace loaned Franklin money in 1730, when the partnership with Meredith went sour. Franklin was now in business on his own.

For the rest of his life, Franklin identified himself as a printer. To get a better idea of what he did, I visit the re-created printing house that the National Park Service runs at 320 Market Street off Franklin Court. The work of a printer was tedious and tiresome. He had to compose his type letter by letter, setting them up backward and upside down, and to do so as quickly and efficiently as possible. A broadsheet the size of the Declaration of Independence required three or four hours of composing work. Franklin recalled one time when he spilled his type after spending hours composing pages. He had to work through the night redoing it but saw the silver lining in the incident, as his neighbors noted his extraordinary work habits, and word of his industry and dedication began to spread.

After setting the type, the printer next applied ink with a device called an inking ball. Made from tree sap, linseed oil, and lamp black, black ink was a sticky substance that adhered well to the metal type. The printer tranferred the ink to the paper by turning a long handle that pressed the paper to the type. He had to repeat the process—inking the type, putting in the paper, and making the impression—for each page, and then he had to set the type for the next page, and the next.

The printing industry has changed tremendously since Franklin's day, but we still use the same terminology. We talk about the press, although its definition has expanded to include television news as well as printed media. Printers kept their capital letters separate in an upper case, giving us the terms for upper- and lower-case letters. Printers minded their "p's and q's," since they looked similar, and a disgruntled printer might be "out of sorts," the sorts being his metal type, which eventually wore out and had to be replaced.

Franklin proved to be a canny businessman, usually to his rivals' ill fortune. After he learned that Andrew Bradford had received a contract from the colonial assembly, he printed the same job himself so that the assemblymen could see how much better his work was. In 1728, Keimer began publishing a newspaper he called *The Universal Instructor in All Arts and Sciences: and Pennsylvania Gazette*, but Franklin kept attacking it with humorous articles in a rival paper. Keimer finally sold the paper to Franklin, who shortened the title to *The Pennsylvania Gazette* and made it a success. Franklin printed the first *Poor Richard's Almanac* in 1732. Thanks in part to its witty sayings, such as "Three may keep a Secret, if two of them are dead," "Love your Neighbor; yet don't pull down your Hedge," and "Fish and Visitors stink in 3 Days," *Poor Richard's* became the most popular almanac in the colonies, selling ten thousand copies annually.

Busy as he was, Franklin found time to create more organizations. Junto members often wanted books to back up the points they made in discussion, so Franklin suggested starting a subscription library. Members would pay to join but then have free access to the library's books. Incorporated on July 1, 1731, the Library Company of Philadelphia had fifty subscribers who paid 40 shillings to join and an additional 10 shillings a year. The fledgling library—the first subscription library in the colonies—solicited book suggestions from James Logan, the Penn family's representative in Pennsylvania, and sent 45 pounds to Peter Collinson, a Quaker merchant in London, to buy its first books. The growing collection moved to the State House in 1739, and it moved again in 1773, this time to a new building called Carpenters' Hall. When

Library Company of Philadelphia

1314 Locust St. ★ (215) 546-3181

www.librarycompany.org

The Library Company of Philadelphia was one of the Junto's first offshoots, and it's still a thriving organization that bills itself as "American's oldest cultural institution," even though both its purpose and its location have changed since Franklin's day. Today it's a research library with headquarters on Locust Street near Rittenhouse Square. The Library Company's collection includes 500,000 printed volumes and 160,000 manuscripts, as well as prints and early American artifacts. The library is open free to the public for research, and a small space hosts changing exhibits. The Reading, Print, and Exhibition Galleries are open from 9 A.M. to 4:45 P.M. Monday through Friday. The library recommends advance appointments to use the Print Room. Visitors interested in Franklin will want to see the Lazzarini statue from the original Library Hall, in a window facing Locust Street, and the old cornerstone above the reception desk. Peter Cooper's 1720 painting of Philadelphia hangs in the Reading Room. The Library Company is next door to the Historical Society of Pennsylvania, at 1300 Locust Street.

Library Hall

105 S. Fifth St. ★ (215) 440-3400

www.amphilsoc.org/about/libhall.htm

The American Philosophical Society's Library Hall re-creates the look of the old Library Company building, complete with a replica of Lazzarini's Franklin statue in a niche above the street. Some items are on exhibition in the hallway areas, which are open to the public Monday through Friday from 9 A.M. to 4:45 P.M.

the First Continental Congress met there a year later, the Library Company granted its members "the use of such Books as they may have occasion for." Both the Second Continental Congress and the Constitutional Convention received the same courtesy.

The library continued to grow. In 1791, it opened brand new quarters on Fifth Street across from the American Philosophical Society. The handsome brick building had a niche above the main entrance that contained a statue of Franklin, garbed in a roman toga and carved from Italian marble by Francesco Lazzarini. In *Life and Times in Colonial Philadelphia*, Joseph N. Kelley says there were stories around town that the statue came to life at night and climbed down in search of the nearest tavern, and that Franklin's grandson, Benjamin Franklin Bache, once stood guard to make sure the statue stayed put.

The library building was torn down in 1887. Today a replica of its original facade, complete with a copy of Lazzarini's statue, adorns the Fifth Street side of the American Philosophical Society's Library Hall, which opened in 1959. The library itself is now in modern quarters at 1314 Locust Street and has the original Lazzarini statue in a picture window at street level. Even if it never came to life, the statue could give a passing drunk the horrors on a dark night—both arms end in stumps, and the features have been eaten away by the elements, making this Franklin look like the ghost of someone who died in a particularly gruesome accident.

Above the reception desk, the library has mounted the cornerstone from the old building. When Franklin wrote the inscription, he kept his name out of it, but the library directors added "at the instance of Benjamin Franklin" in the description of the library's founding. In the reading room beyond, you can find the city Franklin would have seen when he first arrived here. On one wall is the *South East Prospect of the City of Philadelphia*, a painting of the city's waterfront done in 1720 by Peter Cooper. Not much is known about the work, which turned up in a London shop in 1857, but it is the oldest known painting of any North American city.

*Reproduction of Francesco Lazzarini's statue of Franklin
at the American Philosophical Society's Library Hall*

Stenton

4601 N. Eighteenth St. ★ (215) 329-7312

www.stenton.org

James Logan was William Penn's secretary and later the representative for the Penn family in Pennsylvania. A learned, erudite man and a classical scholar, Logan advised the Library Company about what books to purchase. Around 1730, he built a magnificent country home, Stenton, on five hundred acres outside town. At the time of the Revolutionary War's Battle of Germantown, both George Washington and British general William Howe used Stenton as headquarters. The elegant brick Georgian-style house and several outbuildings stand today on three acres of land. Although surrounded by the modern world, Stenton, which never had either electricity or plumbing, still provides a wonderful sense of how the elite lived in eighteenth-century Philadelphia. The estate is in northwest Philadelphia. It's open Tuesday through Saturday from 1 to 4 P.M. and at other times by appointment. Admission is $5 for adults and $4 for seniors and students.

Among the topics the Junto discussed was the danger of fire. Franklin thought that fighting fires required more "Order and Method," so on December 7, 1736, he formed the Union Fire Company, the city's first volunteer unit. Its members provided "a certain Number of Leather Buckets, with strong Bags and Baskets (for packing and transporting of Goods) which were to be brought to every Fire; and we agreed to meet once a Month and spend a social Evening together, in discoursing and communicating such Ideas as occur'd to use upon the Subject of Fires as might be useful in our Conduct on such Occasions."

The Fireman's Hall Museum on Second Street notes Franklin's contributions in its overview of Philadelphia's firefighting history. Children will delight in the various antique fire engines, such as the

*Stained glass window and artifacts
at the Fireman's Hall Museum*

Fireman's Hall Museum

147 N. Second St. ★ (215) 923-1438
www.mfrconsultants.com/pfd/museum.shtml

The Fireman's Hall Museum is in a former firehouse, built in 1876, on Second Street past Elfreth's Alley. Franklin founded Philadelphia's first fire company, and the museum recognizes his contributions as well as those of the firefighters who followed in his footsteps. Children will enjoy the old engines and the re-creation of a fireboat's wheelhouse. The museum also has uniforms, equipment, hats, firemarks, and some impressive stained-glass windows depicting firefighters. There's also a memorial to the New York City firefighters who died in the terrorist attacks on September 11, 2001. Operated by the Philadelphia Fire Department, the museum is free but donations are suggested. It's open Tuesday through Saturday from 9 A.M. to 5 P.M.

Franklin sports a fireman's helmet in this
bas-relief sculpture at a fire station on Arch Street

Philadelphia Contributorship

The Contributorship Companies
212 S. Fourth St. ★ (215) 627-1752
www.contributorship.com

The headquarters of the Philadelphia Contributorship, the insurance company that Franklin helped found in 1752, dates from 1836. It has a small museum that's open to the public Monday through Friday from 9 A.M. to 4 P.M. Items on display include firemarks, firefighter hats, a silver speaking trumpet used to issue orders at fires, and some Franklin artifacts. The building's upstairs rooms are open for tours by appointment only.

American Philosophical Society

104 S. Fifth St. ★ (215) 440-3440

www.amphilsoc.org

The American Philosophical Society completed Philosophical Hall in 1789. Its library in Library Hall across the street is open for qualified researchers. Philosophical Hall has a museum with changing exhibits that is open to the public free of charge. From February 18 until Labor Day, the hours are Thursday through Sunday from 10 A.M. to 4 P.M. From April through Labor Day, it's also open Wednesday evenings from 5 to 8 P.M. From Labor Day until December 11, it's open Friday through Sunday from 10 A.M. to 4 P.M.

1926 American La France pumper, as well as the classic firemen's poles that descend from the upstairs. The museum also has a reproduction of a painting of Franklin wearing a Union Company fireman's hat. A version of this image, with Franklin in profile, graces the side of Engine Company #8 on Arch Street, just down the street from Franklin's grave in the Christ Church Burial Ground.

But forming the Union Fire Company wasn't enough. In 1752, Franklin proposed creation of the Philadelphia Contributorship for the Insurance of Houses from Loss by Fire, which began issuing seven-year policies. Franklin had seat number one on the board, half of whose members belonged to the Union Fire Company.

The company now keeps its headquarters in a stately Federal-style brick building on Fourth Street. The 1836 structure postdates Franklin but has a small museum inside. On one wall is a collection of firemarks, plaques with images of four clasped hands that the company's policyholders attached to their houses. A glass cabinet holds examples of early leather fire buckets and some hats. Another case has articles connected to Franklin, including a snuffbox (although at age eighty-one, Franklin told Dr. Ben-

The American Philosophical Society's Library Hall

jamin Rush that he had never used tobacco in any form, including snuff) and a pair of elaborate shoe buckles that may have been presented to him in France.

Franklin was a born organizer. In 1743, he published *A Proposal for Promoting Useful Knowledge among the British Plantations in America*, which led to the American Philosophical Society, now the country's oldest learned society. Franklin proposed putting the society's headquarters in Philadelphia, then roughly at the midpoint of the thirteen colonies. Members included botanist John Bartram (whose idea it may have been in the first place) and physician Thomas Bond, two men with whom Franklin would have long relationships. Things moved slowly, however, and Franklin complained that the Philadelphia members were "very idle gentlemen." But the society grew and prospered. "We have today over eight hundred members in the society from all walks of life," says Roy Goodman, the society's curator of printed materials (and also president of a society called the Friends of

Franklin). "They run the gamut from Jimmy Carter to Yo-Yo Ma." The society's library today has more than 200,000 bound volumes and 7 million manuscripts. Among its treasures are the journals of Lewis and Clark, first editions of Darwin's *On the Origin of Species* and Newton's *Principia*, an original edition of *Poor Richard's Almanac* from 1737, a treaty with the Indians of the Ohio that Franklin printed in 1747, and the only known copy of "Batchelor's Hall," a poem by Junto member George Webb that Franklin printed in 1731.

The society opened a new brick headquarters next to the State House in 1789, the year before Franklin died, but it's possible he never made it inside. You can, though, because the society has an exhibit space on the first floor that's open to the public.

One of the prime movers behind the society was John Bartram, and it's thanks to him and his son William that you have the opportunity to meet one of Franklin's contemporaries, still alive

Bartram's Garden

Fifty-fourth St. and Lindbergh Blvd.
(215) 729-5281 ★ www.bartramsgarden.org

Bartram's Garden offers a unique rural perspective on city dweller Franklin. His friend, pioneering botanist John Bartram, purchased this land in 1728. You can tour Bartram's somewhat eccentric house or just wander through the gardens and sit by the banks of the Schuylkill River. There is plenty of free parking on the grounds. The gardens are free and open daily (except holidays) from 10 A.M. to 5 P.M. Forty-five-minute house tours leave the gift shop at ten past the hour between noon and 4 P.M. from March through the second week of December. The house is closed Mondays and the last week of the year. Tours are $5 for adults, $4 for seniors, and free for students and children. Reservations are not required for groups of less than ten people.

and well at the ripe old age of 220. It's a ginkgo tree, planted here in 1785 in the gardens that Bartram, a pioneering self-taught botanist, started in 1728. Born a Pennsylvania Quaker in 1699, Bartram traveled throughout the colonies collecting botanical specimens, one of which he named *Franklinia alatamaha* after his friend. John and William discovered the tree in 1765 near the Alatamaha River in Georgia. The tree was last seen in the wild in 1803, and all surviving specimens, including one here in the gardens, are descended from seeds the Bartrams collected.

Bartram's Garden is operated by nonprofit John Bartram Association. To get there, I drive through a downtrodden neighborhood on the west side of the Schuylkill south of the University of Pennsylvania. Finding Bartram's place in the middle of this urban bleakness comes as a surprise, as though these forty-five acres of fields, trees, and gardens have been protected from the encroaching twenty-first century by some kind of force field.

Bartram bought his land here in 1728 and began building a house, an eccentric stone building with three columns and a center wooden section on the side facing the river. A carved inscription below a second-floor window hints at the deistic beliefs that got Bartram drummed out of the Quakers: "It is God Alone, Almighty Lord/The Holy One by Me Ador'd." The house sits on the top of a descending field of gardens that falls to a belt of trees running along the Schuylkill. Tall trees ring the gardens: oaks, London planes, hickories, maples, an American yellowwood from 1809, and the venerable ginkgo. Paths among the trees take you down to the riverside. Sitting on rocks that jut over the Schuylkill in this pastoral oasis, I find it a little jarring to see Philadelphia's skyscrapers on the other side of the river, rising above a cluster of oil tanks.

Bartram, who received an appointment as royal botanist in 1765, hosted Franklin, Washington, and Jefferson here before his death in 1777. In 1980, archeologists discovered another link to Franklin when they dug up the front plate of a Pennsylvania fireplace, commonly known as a Franklin stove. It appears that Bartram used the stove, which dated from the 1760s, to heat his greenhouse.

Franklin Institute

220 N. Twentieth St. ★ (215) 448-1200
http://sln.fi.edu/

Kids of all ages will love the Franklin Institute, which specializes in hands-on, interactive science exhibits and also has a planetarium and an IMAX theater. The Space Command exhibit teaches visitors about the exploration of space; the Franklin Air Show includes planes and a flight simulator; the Sports Challenge examines sports and games and their effects on the body. The 350-ton Baldwin locomotive and giant, walk-through heart are two favorite attractions. In 1976, Congress officially dedicated the Benjamin Franklin National Memorial in the institute's rotunda. Its centerpiece is the huge Franklin statue by James Earle Fraser. There is no charge to visit the memorial. The gift shop is great too. Be prepared to spend several hours at the institute, which is open 9:30 A.M. to 5 P.M. daily. Admission is $13.75 for adults and $11 for children and senior citizens. An additional $5 will include an IMAX film; tickets for IMAX films alone are $9.

Franklin enjoyed the company of men of science like Bartram because he was one himself. His success as a printer allowed him to retire from active business at age forty-two, leaving him more time for scientific experiments. He had always shown an active curiosity and a willingness to experiment. As a boy, he had rigged up a kite that dragged him across a pond, and he also invented crude wooden flippers. In later years, he charted the Gulf Stream, developed bifocals, and recorded observations on everything from the weather to the activities of ants. But how good a scientist was he, really?

"First of all, Franklin never would have called himself a scientist, and other people wouldn't have referred to him as a scientist," says John Alviti, senior curator at the Franklin Institute, the

*Statue of Franklin by James Earle Fraser
at the Franklin Institute*

popular science museum on Benjamin Franklin Parkway. "They would have called him a 'natural philosopher.' And Franklin, like true children of the Enlightenment, believed in rational thinking—that the world was rational, that the world was organized by a series of laws which we only observe, and document our observations."

The Franklin Institute was founded in 1824 to train young men in the industrial arts. Its mission evolved over the years, and in 1934, the institute moved from downtown to its current building. A visit here has become a rite of passage for Philadelphia-area schoolchildren, who take field trips to walk through the giant heart (large enough to fit a 220-foot-tall person) and climb aboard the 350-ton Baldwin locomotive.

The institute's rotunda houses the Benjamin Franklin National Memorial, created by an act of Congress in 1976. Its centerpiece is a huge statue of a seated Franklin, who gazes serenely down on visitors as they enter the building. Sculpted by James Earle Fraser, best known for his design of the Indian head/buffalo nickel, the statue is twenty feet high and weighs thirty tons. The pedestal weighs an additional ninety-two tons. Along one rounded wall are three cases with artifacts that focus on three aspects of Franklin's life: printer, statesman, and scientist.

It's the third role that most interests the Franklin Institute, which has one gallery devoted to Franklin the scientist, called "Franklin . . . He's Electric!" For most Americans, the image of Franklin the scientist is that of an old man flying a kite in a thunderstorm, the most famous electrical experiment in history. Franklin performed his kite experiment when electricity was all the rage. Electrical demonstrations were popular at elegant European parties, where simple devices to generate static electricity sent shocks through the guests' clasped hands, let a man ignite a spoonful of brandy with his finger, or allowed men to exchange "electric kisses" with charged women.

Franklin's interest was sparked on a visit to Boston in 1743, when he met Archibald Spencer, a Scotsman lecturing about electricity and providing demonstrations. "They were imperfectly perform'd, as he was not very expert," Franklin said, but the underlying phenomena fascinated him. He later bought Spencer's equipment. When Peter Collinson, the Quaker merchant in London who acquired books for the Library Company, sent a large glass tube and instructions about how to use it for electrical experiments, Franklin leaped at the opportunity to improve on Spencer's demonstrations.

At the Franklin Institute, Alviti shows me a long, heavy glass tube with a stoppered mouth at one end. I take it from him with some trepidation, for this is the very tube that Collinson sent to Philadelphia. Franklin would fill it with feathers or some such chargeable material, and then rub the tube with a silk cloth until it became charged and the items inside reacted. The experiments that Franklin performed with this simple glass vial sent him down the road to worldwide scientific fame.

Franklin advanced beyond the Collinson tube. The Library Company has a hand-cranked device he used to generate stronger charges that he could store in primitive batteries called Leyden jars. One day in December 1750, he planned to show off his electrical apparatus by using it to kill a turkey and roast it for dinner, but in this case the turkey had the last laugh. Franklin accidentally completed the circuit himself when he grasped a chain connecting his two charged jars, and the shock knocked him cold. "I am Ashamed to have been Guilty of so Notorious A Blunder," he wrote to his brother John.

Alviti points out that the electricity Franklin experimented with was static electricity, not the electromagnetic electricity that comes from our wall plugs. "What did that give us?" he asks. "Well, he gave us a language to talk about the physical properties of electricity, the notion of positive and negative, and he used the word 'fluid' in describing electricity."

Franklin's writings about his experiments attracted attention in Europe. He noticed the similarities between static electricity and lightning and suggested an experiment in which a pointed metal rod could draw lightning from the sky. Before Franklin did the experiment himself, Frenchmen successfully performed what they called "the Philadelphia Experiment" outside Paris.

Sometime before he heard the news from France, probably in June 1752, Franklin performed his kite experiment. Or did he? Franklin's own accounts of the event were sketchy. Joseph Priestley, an English scientist who eventually moved to Pennsylvania, provided the most thorough account in 1767, evidently based on what Franklin told him. Some people interpret the lack of direct proof as evidence that Franklin made the whole thing up. Local legend says that Franklin most certainly did perform the kite experiment, and that he did it on the site of present-day Loxley Court, a secluded row of residential buildings just off Arch Street. These stories say that carpenter Benjamin Loxley provided the famous key that Franklin suspended from his kite string to draw the electrical charge.

Modern Philadelphia commemorates Franklin and his kite with *Bolt of Lightning . . . A Memorial to Benjamin Franklin*, a giant stainless steel sculpture by Isamu Noguchi that stands at the end

Bolt of Lightning . . . A Memorial to Benjamin Franklin

This giant sculpture, 101 feet high and weighing 60 tons, stands on an urban island between Franklin Square and the Benjamin Franklin Bridge. Isamu Noguchi conceived the sculpture in the 1930s but couldn't realize his vision until 1984. It's not easy to reach—you'll have to bolt through traffic that zips around the sculpture on the approach to the bridge.

In 2006, a citywide storytelling program, Once Upon a Nation, will open Heritage Fair at Franklin Square, which will also include a carousel, mini-golf, playgrounds, and crafts. The summer-long storytelling program debuted in 2005, with thirteen benches that featured performers specially trained at a three-week "Benstitute." It is a joint production of Historic Philadelphia, Inc., Independence National Historical Park, and other organizations. See www.onceuponanation.org.

of the Benjamin Franklin Bridge. Supported by posts and cables, the semiabstract sculpture, depicting a kitelike object balanced atop a large key, soars into the sky and draws your gaze up with it. I wouldn't want to stand beneath it during a thunderstorm, though.

Franklin knew about the danger of lightning, and he did something about it by inventing the lightning rod. Alviti shows me a piece of bent, rusted metal from one of Franklin's first light-

---

Christ Church

Second St. above Market. St. ★ (215) 922-1695
www.christchurchphila.org
or www.oldchristchurch.org

Christ Church is just off Market Street off Second. Franklin occasionally attended services here, but Deborah Franklin was the real churchgoer in the family. In 1737, when someone stole Deborah's prayer book from her pew here, her husband placed a notice in his newspaper: "The person who took it is desired to open it and read the Eighth Commandment, and afterwards return it into the same pew again; upon which no further notice will be taken." Franklin helped organize the lottery that raised money for the two-hundred-foot steeple in 1754. Several of his acquaintances are buried on the church grounds, including Andrew Hamilton, a lawyer who served as a mentor to young Ben and designed Independence Hall; Ann, the wife of Sir William Keith, the governor who sent Franklin to London with false promises; and poetess and salon hostess Elizabeth Graeme, who was William Franklin's first love. Today Christ Church is an active Episcopalian place of worship. Tours are given throughout the day, Monday through Saturday from 9 A.M. to 5 P.M. and Sunday from 12:30 to 5 P.M. A donation of $2 for adults and $1 for students is suggested.

Christ Church steeple

ning rods, which had been installed on the Wister House at 141 High (now Market) Street around 1749. It was probably bent, Alviti said, by a lightning strike.

Alviti tells me that King George III of England, who also dabbled in science, advocated a blunt lightning rod, unlike Franklin's with its pointed, needlelike tip. "That was another issue between the two," Alviti says, "besides the important one of whether America should separate from the British." Who was right, the king or the natural philosopher? "That issue has been debated for a long, long time, and only recently have scientists come up with data that suggests one was better than the other." And the winner, in this contest at least, was George III.

It's possible that Franklin delayed performing his own "Philadelphia experiment" because he was waiting for completion of the Christ Church steeple. The elegant two-hundred-foot spire remains one of Philadelphia's most distinctive landmarks and a visual reminder of Franklin's impact on the city, for he helped organize a lottery to fund it in 1754. Tickets cost about 1 pound, and 15 percent of the proceeds went to the steeple's cost, ultimately raising two-thirds of the 3,000-pound price tag.

Founded in 1695 on a plot of land on Second Street just north of Market Street, the church had started as an Anglican stronghold in a Quaker-dominated city. As Quaker power waned in Philadelphia, Christ Church became increasingly important even as its first building deteriorated. Construction on the new building began in 1727 and proceeded in stages for seventeen years, with another ten passing before the steeple was completed. There's no record of any architect, although it was designed in the style of London's Christopher Wren. A solid Georgian structure with wood trim and two floors of arched windows along its sides, the church boasts an ornate Palladian window on its east end. The building's brickwork was done in Flemish bond with "blew headers," a technique in which some of the bricks were laid end-on and glazed blue. The glazing was pure adornment, says Neil Ronk, the head guide at the church. "To some degree, the Flemish bond speaks to the grandeur of the church. When it was just finished, it would have literally glittered and glistened in the sun."

Franklin attended church here on occasion, but he was not a regular churchgoer. In Boston, he wrote, "[My] indiscrete Disputations about Religion began to make me pointed at with Horror by good People, as an Infidel or Atheist." Although Franklin may not have attended regularly, this was the right church for him, the place where an ambitious man could go to socialize with other rising young men. "This was a church where you could see and be seen," Ronk says. According to Ronk, the relationship between the church and Franklin was emblematic of their city and the times. "If you ever wanted to get an idea of what Philadelphia thought of, not just in Mr. Franklin's mind, but the Philadelphia of Mr. Franklin, you'd be hard-pressed to get a better institution than this. This is in a wonderful sense the structure of the hubris of Franklin's Philadelphia, the sense of confidence, the sense of anything is possible. The building is, upon its completion—finished in 1754—the tallest building in America for seventy-five

University of Pennsylvania

University of Pennsylvania Information Center
Thirty-fourth St. and Locust St. ★ www.upenn.edu

A marker on a Fourth Street parking garage between Arch Street and Market Street notes the location of the building Franklin helped establish "for the use of any preacher of any religious persuasion who might desire to say something to the people at Philadelphia." The building later housed the academy that Franklin founded, which evolved into the University of Pennsylvania. In 1980, the university's class of 1930 erected a plaque on the corner of Arch Street and Fourth Street to commemorate their school's founder.

Today the University of Pennsylvania is on the west side of the Schuylkill River and offers all the amenities of a thriving academic community, plus several statues of Franklin. Online, the University Library has an evolving presence called "Penn in the Age of Franklin" at sceti.library.upenn.edu/franklin/index.cfm.

years. This is Philadelphia when we thought we were the London of the New World."

To truly be the "London of the New World," Philadelphia needed an institution of higher learning. Naturally, Franklin was at the forefront of the effort to create one. In 1749, he wrote and published an anonymous pamphlet titled *Proposals Relating to the Education of Youth in Pennsylvania*, in which he proposed the creation of an academy. The school opened for business later that year in a rented warehouse, with Franklin as the president of the board of trustees. Over the years, the institution flourished and changed. Today it is the University of Pennsylvania.

The academy quickly outgrew its first rented building, but thanks to Franklin, a new building already existed for it. When Philadelphia's established churches had shut their doors to a

Statue of Franklin by George W. Lundeen
at the University of Pennsylvania

charismatic Anglican preacher named George Whitefield, the action spurred Franklin to raise money to construct a building "so that even if the Mufti of Constantinople were to send a missionary to preach Mohammedanism to us, he would find a pulpit at his service." A parking garage on Fourth Street next to the Holiday Inn stands there now, but a plaque marks the spot.

Franklin's experience with the academy was not a happy one. He wanted to provide a practical education to serve artisans and middle-class students, but other trustees insisted on a traditional, classical education of Latin and Greek more suitable for the moneyed elite. Franklin lost the battle to the classical proponents, one of whom was William Smith, the man Franklin picked to lead the school. Smith was a hardheaded, hard-drinking, ambitious Scotsman who became a continual thorn in Franklin's side. "I made that Man my Enemy by doing him too much Kindness," Franklin wrote of Smith. "And since 'tis convenient to have at least one

Enemy, who by his Readiness to revile one on all Occasions may make one careful of one's Conduct, I shall keep him an Enemy for that purpose. . . ." In 1756, Franklin's differences with other board members led to his removal as president, a decision that hurt him deeply. "The Trustees had reap'd the full Advantage of my Head, Hands, Heart and Purse, in getting through the first Difficulties of the Design, and when they thought they could do without me, they laid me aside," he wrote years later.

But time heals all wounds, especially when the combatants have been dead for centuries. The University of Pennsylvania now has a 269-acre campus on the other side of the Schuylkill River, but it hasn't forgotten its ties to Franklin. He sits on a bench at the corner of a shady pedestrian passage called Locust Walk, reading a copy of *The Pennsylvania Gazette* dated May 16, 1987. Designed by George W. Lundeen and given to the university as a gift by the class of 1962, this playful statue, which has a bronze pigeon perched on the bench, has become a much-photographed Philadelphia landmark. Farther down Locust

Thomas Bond House

129 S. Second St.
(215) 923-8523 *or* (800) 845-2663
www.winston-salem-inn.com/philadelphia

Thomas Bond, Franklin's friend and the man who approached him with the idea of starting a hospital, was born in Maryland and received medical training in Paris. He was an original member of the American Philosophical Society and a leading figure in Pennsylvania's medical history. In 1769, Bond built a four-story house on Second Street. It remained a residence until 1810, and then housed everything from a tannery to a retail shop. Now it's a bed-and-breakfast. Guests have a choice of twelve rooms, including the Benjamin Franklin and the William Penn.

Walk is another Franklin, seated atop a pedestal in front of Gothic College Hall. He appears to be staring quizzically across the way at a Claes Oldenburg and Coosje van Bruggen sculpture of a large, broken button. This Franklin, created by Philadelphia sculptor John J. Boyle, was a gift of department store magnate Justus C. Strawbridge in 1899. According to one story, Oldenburg and van Bruggen made their sculpture in response to a joke that Boyle's Franklin was paunchy enough to pop a button.

The university has a third statue, one of young Ben striding into Philadelphia in 1723, at Weightman Hall on Thirty-third Street, near Locust. The work of R. Tait McKenzie, the school's first professor of physical education, it was a gift from the class of 1904.

Not content with starting libraries, academies, and learned societies, Franklin also became involved in the creation of the first hospital in the colonies. In 1750, he received a visit from Dr. Thomas

Pennsylvania Hospital

800 Spruce St. ★ (215) 829-5434
www.pennhealth.com/pahosp/

Pennsylvania Hospital was the first hospital in the North American colonies. The original Pine Building contains the cornerstone, protected under plastic, with the inscription that Franklin wrote. The moat around the building is where hospital attendants once exercised mentally ill patients. This is still a working—and very busy—hospital, but you can take guided or self-guided tours Monday through Friday from 9 A.M. to 4 P.M. (you can also take self-guided tours on Saturday). You must call ahead, (215) 829-3270, to reserve a guided tour. All tours meet at the Welcome Desk through the main entrance on Eighth Street. You can pick up an informative brochure at the desk. The hospital asks that you follow the rules set by their forefathers, to wit: no profane language, no gambling, and no spitting on the floors.

Bond, a friend and one of the American Philosophical Society's original members. Bond had studied medicine in Paris and London and had been trying to raise money to found a hospital in Philadelphia, with little success. Finally he turned to his friend Franklin, who had the reputation as the go-to man for things of this sort. "I am often ask'd by those to whom I propose Subscribing, Have you consulted Franklin upon this Business?" Bond told him. "And when I tell them that I have not, (supposing it rather out of your Line) they do not subscribe but say they will consider it."

Franklin said he would help out. He wrote pieces for his *Pennsylvania Gazette* advocating the hospital and approached his many acquaintances for funds. He also petitioned the Pennsylvania Assembly, proposing that if he could raise donations of 2,000 pounds, the assembly would appropriate an equal amount. The assembly agreed to the scheme. As Franklin put it, "The Members who had oppos'd the Grant, and now conceiv'd they might have the Credit of being charitable without the Expense, agreed to its Passage. . . ." But they had underestimated Franklin's fund-raising abilities. It was perhaps history's first example of matching funds.

The cornerstone for the east wing of the Pennsylvania Hospital was laid on May 28, 1755. Franklin wrote its inscription, still visible on the stone, which lies beneath a protective plastic cover below some stairs:

In the year of Christ MDCCLV
George the Second happily reigning
(For he sought the happiness of his people)
Philadelphia flourishing
(For its inhabitants were publick spirited)
This building
By the bounty of the government
And of many private persons
Was piously founded
For the relief of the sick and miserable
May the God of Mercies
Bless this undertaking.

When it came time to elect a board of directors in June, Franklin was selected as president. At that time, the hospital was considered to be on the outskirts of town. Nonetheless, entertainment-deprived Philadelphians came out to watch the insane patients being taken out for exercise. It became such a craze that the hospital began charging admission. Today the hospital lies in the city's heart, and like Philadelphia in general, it's grown a great deal. Approaching the busy main entrance, buzzing with arrivals and departures, you can see the original cupola rising behind it. In 1765, a sailor named Thomas Perrine escaped from his cell and climbed into the cupola. Hospital personnel couldn't get him down, so they let him live there, and he stayed for nine years, growing increasingly hermitlike in appearance, with long, matted hair and beard and daggerlike nails.

The hospital offers tours, either on your own or with a guide. I choose to guide myself, so I pick up a brochure at the welcome desk in the modern portion, then make my way through the busy

The Great Court at the Pennsylvania Hospital

*Bust of Franklin in the library
at the Pennsylvania Hospital*

hospital. It's a somewhat disjointed feeling, seeking eighteenth-century history in a modern medical facility, but then I round a corner and find Benjamin West's epic painting of *Christ Healing the Sick in the Temple*. West was an expatriate Pennsylvanian who studied in Philadelphia but spent most of his life in Europe and died in London. He never forgot his connection with Philadelphia, however. In 1767, he sent the mummified hand of an Egyptian princess for the collections of Franklin's Library Company, and toward the end of his life, he promised this painting as a gift to the hospital. He ended up painting two versions. The first one created such a sensation in England that West, strapped for funds, sold it to Britain's National Gallery.

Stepping off the carpeted surface of the modern hospital into the Great Court of the old building is like stepping out of a time machine. The court, completed in 1804, has a floor of elegant Portuguese tile. Curved staircases lined with marble memorials rise in hushed solemnity. A bust of Franklin sits on one table; he almost appears to be looking at something that surely would have attracted his attention, a hand-pumped fire engine that the hospital purchased in 1803.

There's another Franklin bust upstairs in the hospital's historic library, a dark, narrow room that is quiet except for the whir of the air conditioners that keep the historic volumes at a constant temperature. It's not all books, though. There's also a jar containing a seven-pound tumor that Dr. Philip Syng Physick, the grandson of Franklin's good friend Philip Syng, removed from the face of James Hayes on Christmas Day in 1805.

Upstairs, I step into another bit of surgery's past, a neat, round room that is grisly only through implication. This is the nation's first surgical amphitheater, in use from 1804 until 1868. A skylight offered the only good light in these days before electricity, and surgeons could operate only in the bright sun available between 11 A.M. and 2 P.M. Until the 1840s, the doctors used no anesthesia; until the 1890s they didn't bother with any sterilization.

The hospital and other organizations were just some of Franklin's activities during this busy period, as he became increasingly involved in government and politics. He worked to improve the city watch, and hired a street sweeper to keep the dirt streets under control, and even designed an improved lamp for street lighting, copies of which are still being used in Philadelphia today. In 1736, he became clerk to the Pennsylvania Assembly, the colony's representative body. A year later, he became Philadelphia's postmaster, and in 1753, he became the deputy postmaster for all of British North America. He became Philadelphia councilman in 1748, justice of the peace in 1749, and an alderman in 1751, the same year he was elected a member of the assembly. During the French and Indian War, Franklin commanded detachments that constructed forts on the Pennsylvania frontier, and in 1756, he received a commission as a colonel in the militia.

It was a turbulent time for Pennsylvania politics, and Franklin thrust himself into the center of affairs. The assembly often clashed with the governor, who spoke for the proprietors, the descendants of William Penn who still owned the colony. The assembly wanted to tax the proprietors' lands to help defray

Lights of Liberty

Sixth St. and Chestnut St.
(215) 542-3789 *or* (877) 462-1776
www.lightsofliberty.org

Billed as "A Revolution in Sound and Light," Lights of Liberty is an audio-visual walking tour that tells the story of Philadelphia's Revolutionary War history among its actual buildings. Huge projectors cast images on walls while high-tech headphones provide accompanying sound, including the voices of Walter Cronkite, Charlton Heston, and Ossie Davis. One of the vignettes takes place in Franklin Court and tells the story of Deborah Franklin's defense of her home during the Stamp Act disturbances. It is stirring to see the huge projected text of the Declaration of Independence scroll across the face of Independence Hall while the Philadelphia Orchestra provides a rousing soundtrack. Admission is $17.76 for adults, $16 for seniors and students, and $12 for children, who can listen to a separate program geared to them. Show dates and times vary seasonally; it's best to check the website before you visit. While you wait in the lobby for your tour, you can ask questions of Ben Franklin's ghost, played by Ralph Archbold.

the costs of the French and Indian War. The proprietors refused to allow it. In 1757, the assembly appointed Franklin as its agent in England to negotiate with the British government over the issue. That June, Franklin and his son William left port in New York for London. Deborah, who refused to board a ship, remained behind.

Franklin remained in London for five years, living with a surrogate family of landlady Margaret Stevenson and her daughter, Polly, on London's Craven Street. He made some progress in the assembly's case against the proprietors. For his part, William managed to get himself named the royal governor of New Jersey. On a visit to Scotland in 1759, Franklin received an honorary degree from St. Andrews University and from then on was often addressed as Doctor Franklin. When it came time to leave Britain, he found it difficult to tear himself away. He wrote a friend that if he could persuade Deborah to cross the ocean with him, he might settle permanently in London. Finally, in August 1762, he somewhat reluctantly headed back across the Atlantic to the political turmoil in Pennsylvania.

Franklin's image today may be of a humorous and benevolent elder statesman, but his political enemies saw him as anything but lovable. Gov. John Penn, William Penn's grandson, loathed Franklin and feared his growing power in Philadelphia. "There will never be any prospect of ease and happiness while that Villain has the liberty of Spreading about the poison of that inveterate Malice and ill Nature, which is so deeply implanted in his own black heart," Penn wrote to his uncle Thomas back in London.

Such personal animosities spilled over into politics. After a particularly nasty and brutal campaign in the fall of 1764, Franklin lost his seat in the assembly, but the assembly quickly voted to send him back to London as its agent. He sailed in November, not knowing that he would never see his wife again, nor return to Philadelphia for more than ten years.

Before he left, Franklin commissioned Robert Smith, one of the best architects in the colonies, to build him a house in a courtyard off Market Street. The house was still in its early stages when Franklin left, but he followed its progress through letters from Deborah. Even from London, Franklin tried to control the house's construction, explaining to his wife, for instance, how to handle the kitchen's exhaust system, "as it is a mere Machine, and being new to you, I think you will scarce know how to work it."

Not that Deborah couldn't handle things herself. After passage of the Stamp Act in 1765, she had to literally hold down the fort. Franklin had argued against the Stamp Act in London but decided that opposing it "would have been as useless as stopping the sun from setting." In an uncharacteristic misreading of Colonial sentiment, Franklin even recommended a friend as revenue collector, not realizing how much the tax had angered his countrymen. In Philadelphia, rumors spread that Franklin had advocated passage of the Stamp Act, and angry mobs threatened the house in Franklin Court. Deborah borrowed some guns and prepared to defend her home. As she reported to her husband, "If aney one came to disturbe me I wold show a proper resentement and I shold be very much afrunted." But the mob had second thoughts and spared Franklin's new house. "I honour much the Spirit and Courage you show'd and the prudent Preparations you made in that Time of Danger," Deborah's husband wrote her. "That Woman deserves a good House that is determined to defend it."

Benjamin Franklin in 1785, by Charles Willson Peale.

Statesman

Back in London, Franklin returned to his old quarters on Craven Street. Philadelphia artist Charles Willson Peale called on him there in 1767 and found Franklin kissing a young woman, perhaps a maid, who was sitting on his knee. According to one account, Franklin didn't see Peale, who discretely retreated downstairs before clattering his way noisily back up. The artist made a drawing of the scene in his diary.

Happy as his domestic situation was, Franklin was distressed to watch the gulf widening between the colonies and Britain. At the end of 1772, to show that the problem lay not with the king but with his advisors, he leaked letters written by Massachusetts governor Thomas Hutchinson advocating harsh treatment of the colonies. Two men embroiled in the controversy engaged in a duel before Franklin admitted his role in the affair. He was called before the Privy Council in January 1774 for a session marked by much personal abuse, which Franklin endured stoically. The council stripped him of his post as postmaster general and left open the possibility that Franklin would be arrested.

The year 1774 was not a good one. The previous December, Boston had protested the British Parliament's actions with its Tea

Party, and in the spring, the British government passed a series of acts designed to punish Boston for the affair. On the personal side, Franklin and his son William, now New Jersey's governor, were drifting apart. "You, who are a thorough Courtier, see every thing with Government Eyes," Franklin chided him in September. The heaviest blow hit in December, with the death of Deborah, whose health had deteriorated following a stroke and was not improved by her husband's long absence. Still, Franklin remained in London until March 1775, when he finally sailed home.

He returned to a country that had fallen over the brink from protest into rebellion. Minutemen and redcoats clashed at Lexington and Concord in April. The gulf that Franklin had watched widen inexorably while he was in England had now become unbridgeable.

Franklin reached Philadelphia on May 5, after a decade's absence, and was immediately in the center of the whirlwind as he attempted to catch up with old friends and new political developments. He could have learned about both at the elegant brick home of Samuel and Elizabeth Powel on South Third Street, where evidence on the walls shows that he visited in 1775.

Samuel Powel was both the last Colonial mayor of Philadelphia and the first American one. A member of the city's wealthy elite, Powel had spent several years on a grand tour of Europe after he graduated from the College of Philadelphia in 1759. Upon his return to Philadelphia, he purchased this three-story brick house from an unlucky merchant who had suffered business reverses after commissioning it. Money was no object for Powel, who owned about ninety properties throughout the city.

The Powel House, which is operated today by the Philadelphia Society for the Preservation of Landmarks, has a number of Franklin connections. Powel used the front room as an office, and in it there's an apothecary scale that Franklin allegedly sent him from London. "Apparently they had struck up their friendship again while Powel was on his grand European tour," says the society's J. Del Conner. "As I understand it, when Powel returned to Philadelphia, he had written to Franklin complaining about being shortchanged in coin from people who came to pay their rent and

Powel House

244 S. Third St. ★ (215) 627-0364
www.philalandmarks.org

Samuel Powel was the last mayor of Philadelphia during the Colonial era and the first one under an American government. Born a Quaker but the inheritor of his family's fortune, he eventually cast off the plain religion of the Friends and converted to the more luxury-accepting Church of England. He married Elizabeth Willing in August 1769 and the young and wealthy couple established a genteel, sophisticated home with many furnishings purchased during Samuel's grand tour of Europe. Today the house is open to the public under the auspices of the Philadelphia Society for the Preservation of Landmarks. Tours are given Thursday through Saturday from noon to 5 P.M. and Sunday from 1 to 5 P.M., with the last tour at 4 P.M. Admission is $5 for adults, $4 for seniors and students, $3 per person for tours of ten or more, and a family rate of $12.

Physick House

321 S. Fourth St. ★ (215) 925-7866
www.philalandmarks.org

The society also operates the Physick House, home of Dr. Philip Syng Physick, the "father of American surgery." He built his townhouse in 1786; today it includes a small medical museum. Hours and admission fees are the same as for the Powel House.

things. They had been clipped—you'd shave a little off the edge—that's where 'clip joint' comes from. And in response, Franklin sent him this apothecary scale to weigh his coins." As Poor Richard might have said, a penny weighed is a penny earned.

The Powel House

The spacious ballroom upstairs has an elaborate mantle carved with Aesop's fable of the fox and the grapes (this is a reproduction; the original is in the Philadelphia Museum of Art). On display in the ballroom is a copy of a letter Sally Franklin wrote to her father after attending a ball here in 1779 to celebrate George and Martha Washington's twentieth wedding anniversary, saying that Washington inquired "after you in the most affectionate manner and speaks of you highly."

The most interesting bit of Franklinania in the Powel House is in the upstairs chamber, called the Withdrawing Room. According to Conner, in the spring of 1775, Franklin, Washington, and Washington's younger brother, John Augustine, visited Samuel Powel, who traced their silhouettes. Those silhouettes now hang on the walls. Washington, according to legend, didn't like his. "It's marked on the back, 'not a good likeness,'" says Conner, probably because Powel included Washington's double chin.

Washington was soon off to Cambridge to take command of the Continental Army. Franklin remained in Philadelphia as a delegate to the Second Continental Congress, which was meeting in Pennsylvania's State House. Franklin never referred to this formal Georgian building on Chestnut between Fifth Street and Sixth Street as Independence Hall. Not until long after his death, when the Marquis de Lafayette returned to the United States for a triumphal tour in 1824, did people begin referring to it by that name. To Franklin, it was always the State House.

From the Chestnut Street side, Independence Hall seems to crouch at the edge of the sidewalk as though afraid of calling attention to itself in the middle of the busy modern city that rises above it. The building is more expansive on the opposite side, where it faces the green space of Independence Square. The bell tower, added to this side in 1752, gives the central building a better sense of confidence and grandeur. Here it truly becomes Independence Hall, the birthplace of the United States of America.

Franklin had all kinds of ties to this building. Andrew Hamilton, who sketched out the rough design for the new State House when he was speaker of the assembly in 1732, was a mentor for

Independence National Historical Park

143 S. Third St. ★ (215) 965-2305

www.nps.gov/inde/

Independence Visitor Center

Sixth St. and Market St.

(800) 537-7676 *or* (215) 965-7676

www.independencevisitorcenter.com

The National Park Service operates several historic sites in Philadelphia under the umbrella of Independence National Historic Park, which includes Independence Hall, the Liberty Bell Center, Franklin Court, Declaration House, and several other places. The best place to coordinate a visit to this rich trove of Colonial and Revolutionary history is at the Independence Visitor Center at the corner of Sixth Street and Market Street. The center offers orientation films, a gift shop, computer kiosks, and brochures by the dozens. It is open daily from 8:30 A.M. to 7 P.M. from July 1 through September 4, and 8:30 A.M. to 5 P.M. the rest of the year.

The Visitor Center is also where you get the tickets required between March and December for tours of Independence Hall. The tours take place every fifteen minutes. Tickets are free, but it's a good idea to arrive early during the busier months, before all the day's tickets have been handed out. For a small service charge, you can reserve tickets online up to a year in advance at reservations.nps.gov. Tickets are not required for the Liberty Bell Center, but you have to go through the same security entrance, which can take some time. Both Independence Hall and the Liberty Bell Center are open daily from 9 A.M. to 5 P.M.

Even if you don't have Independence Hall tickets, you can still visit the "Great Essentials" exhibit, Congress Hall, and Old City Hall. Housed in Independence Hall's West

Wing, "Great Essentials" includes copies of the Declaration of Independence, the Articles of Confederation, and the Constitution, as well as the Philip Syng inkwell purportedly used by signers of the Declaration and Constitution. Next door is Congress Hall, where Congress met when Philadelphia was the nation's capital from 1790 to 1800. George Washington and John Adams were both inaugurated as president here, although Washington's first inauguration was in New York. Next to Independence Hall's East Wing is Old City Hall, where the U.S. Supreme Court met from 1791 until 1800.

The National Park Service also operates a re-creation of the Graff House, where Thomas Jefferson wrote the Declaration of Independence in a rented room, on the corner of Market Street and Seventh Street. It contains a re-creation of the house's bedroom and parlor, along with some exhibits about Jefferson and the Declaration.

The Todd House, at Fourth Street and Walnut Street, is where the future Dolley Madison lived when she was married to lawyer John Todd, who died of yellow fever in 1793. The Bishop White House, at number 309 Walnut Street, was home to the onetime rector of Christ Church. Both houses are part of Independence National Historical Park and are open to the public, but for tours only. You can make arrangements for tours at the Visitor Center. Between the buildings is a beautiful re-creation of an eighteenth-century garden.

The National Park Service's old visitor center has been converted into the Independence Living History Center. Visitors can watch through large windows as archeologists work on objects recovered from various digs around Philadelphia. The center is at Third Street and Chestnut Street, and also hosts screenings of the musical *1776*.

Independence Hall

PHOTO BY KYLE WEAVER

young Franklin and steered government printing work his way. Franklin worked here when he became clerk to the Pennsylvania Assembly in 1736 and as an assemblyman starting in 1751. He performed electrical demonstrations in the State House, and the Library Company kept its collections in the west wing beginning in 1739.

The building Hamilton designed was a formal, two-story Georgian structure, solidly constructed of brick, with an east and a west wing joined by open piazzas. Georgian architecture called for strict attention to symmetry; two windows on the first floor, required to preserve the building's visual balance, are behind walls on the inside. The first floor held the Assembly Room and the Supreme Court; upstairs was a commodious Long Room for official functions plus two smaller chambers. (Starting in 1802, the Long Room housed Charles Willson Peale's museum of art and natural science.) The State House did not get its distinctive steeple until 1753; it housed a bell the assembly had ordered two years earlier.

Franklin certainly knew the sound of this bell. It summoned him to meetings of the assembly, and he heard it ringing for important events from its perch in the State House steeple.

Because of its biblical inscription to "proclaim liberty throughout the land unto all the inhabitants thereof," the State House bell has become a symbol of freedom known as the Liberty Bell. It was cast at London's Whitechapel Foundry, and it cracked the first time it was tested in Philadelphia. Local craftsmen recast it, though it took them a couple tries to get it right. The bell cracked again in 1846, and workmen drilled out the fracture so that the edges wouldn't rub against each other and ruin the tone. It didn't help. Later that year, probably while ringing to celebrate Washington's Birthday, the bell cracked again, leaving a hairline fracture that extends up and across from the top of the large gash. The old story that the bell cracked tolling for the funeral of Supreme Court chief justice John Marshall is not true, nor is the myth that the bell tolled to announce the adoption of the Declaration of Independence on July 4, 1776. By then the State

The Liberty Bell and Independence Hall
PHOTO BY KYLE WEAVER

House's steeple had rotted so badly that ringing the bell would have been dangerous. The steeple was torn down in 1781 and not replaced until 1828.

The bell traveled extensively throughout the United States until 1915, when it returned to Philadelphia for the last time. It was on display in Independence Hall until the early 1970s, when it was moved to its own pavilion in time for the Bicentennial. In 2003, the bell moved into new and roomier quarters across

Chestnut Street from Independence Hall. The structure was erected on the site of the slaves' quarters of the house George Washington used when he was president. That was a sad irony, because the abolitionist movement adopted the bell as its symbol in the 1830s. Some local historians accused the Park Service of covering up this unpleasant aspect of the American story, and the Park Service later agreed to include material about slavery in Philadelphia at the site.

After passing through stringent security, I make my way through the exhibits in the long, snakelike structure. The Liberty Bell sits at the building's end, like a guru on a mountaintop, in front of a huge picture window overlooking Independence Hall. After such a buildup, the bell seems almost too small to contain its metaphorical weight. Its base is rough, its body pitted and etched. I can see the drill marks in the large crack, and the smaller crack radiating away from it like a network of veins. It's hard not to feel a surge of patriotism when confronted by this famous symbol. From a nearby exhibit, I can hear John Philip Sousa's "Liberty Bell March." The fact that this served as the theme song for "Monty Python's Flying Circus" lessens the solemnity a bit.

Franklin had hardly set foot in Philadelphia before he was back in the State House as a delegate to the Second Continental Congress. Although a case of the gout kept him from attending regularly, he was appointed to the committee assigned to draft a document declaring the colonies' independence from Britain. He may have provided some suggestions to Virginia delegate Thomas Jefferson, who actually wrote the document in a rented room not far from the State House. One of Franklin's suggestions may have been to change "we hold these truths to be sacred and undeniable" to "we hold these truths to be self-evident." And he consoled Jefferson, who was upset over Congress' editing, with the story of a hatmaker whose friends criticized the wording of his sign until all it contained was the man's name and the picture of a hat.

On July 2, 1776, Congress voted for independence. Two days later, it formally adopted the Declaration of Independence, which Sheriff John Nixon read publicly for the first time on July 8 in the park now called Independence Square. You can see Nixon's copy in the "Great Essentials" exhibit in Independence Hall's West Wing. The delegates did not sign the Declaration until August 2, when Franklin supposedly quipped, "We must all hang together, or most assuredly, we shall all hang separately." Franklin's close friend Philip Syng made the inkstand the signers used, which is also on display in the same exhibit. To me it looks like a salt-and-pepper shaker with a bottle opener in the center.

Franklin was also a member of the Congress's Committee of Secret Correspondence. In that capacity, he met a French envoy, Julien-Alexandre Achard de Bonvouloir, at Carpenters' Hall in December 1775. It was a tentative start to the delicate negotiations for an alliance with France.

Carpenters' Hall would have been new to Franklin, having been completed only the year before he returned to Philadelphia as the headquarters of the Carpenters' Company, a craft guild. The company had invited the First Continental Congress to use

Carpenters' Hall

320 Chestnut St. ★ (215) 925-0167
www.carpentershall.org

Carpenters' Hall, built between 1770 and 1774, was the headquarters of the Carpenters' Company, a craft guild. Its members included Robert Smith, who built Franklin's house and many of Philadelphia's finest structures, and Thomas Procter, who built City Tavern. Delegates to the First Continental Congress elected to meet here instead of the State House (today's Independence Hall) because they wanted to avoid the influence of the conservative Pennsylvania Assembly. Carpenters' Hall is still owned by the Carpenters' Company, but it is open to the public from Tuesday through Sunday (Wednesday through Sunday in January and February) from 10 A.M. to 4 P.M. There is no admission charge. If you're lucky, you will be there for one of the daily demonstrations of Franklin's glass armonica.

Carpenters' Hall

the building in 1774, when it probably still smelled of paint and
fresh wood. Perhaps the new building inspired some members
to start thinking about constructing a new country.

When I visit Carpenters' Hall, the neat, compact brick building is filled not with political debate, but with the ethereal sounds

of a glass armonica, a musical instrument Franklin invented in London. A great music lover, he had delighted in the sounds made by rubbing a wet finger around the rim of a wineglass. To improve on wineglasses, he mounted glass cylinders of varying sizes on a central rod. The player rotated the rod by pumping a pedal and created notes by pressing wet fingertips against the bowls. The instrument became popular in Europe, and Mozart and Beethoven even composed music for it.

One of Mozart's pupils was his blind cousin, Marianne Kirchgaessner, who studied with the composer for four years. Today in Carpenters' Hall, Carolinn Skyler plays the instrument in the character of Kirchgaessner. Skyler too is blind, but unlike Kirchgaessner, she gets a little help from an electric motor that rotates the spindle for her. Skyler plays "Greensleeves," and the music is otherworldly, as fragile as the glass bowls that make it. "Amazing Grace" is next, and then Skyler plays the aria from Mozart's *Magic Flute* and an air Mozart composed specifically for the armonica. I've heard nothing like it before and can understand why eighteenth-century audiences fell under the instrument's spell.

But the armonica soon fell out of favor, with some people saying the tones drove its players mad. Perhaps that was because a French doctor tried using the armonica to cure insanity, or maybe, as some have theorized, the lead-based paint on the rims of the glass bowls afflicted players with lead poisoning. That would have been somewhat ironic, as Franklin was among the first people to suggest that lead had toxic effects.

Lead poisoning of a different kind would kill many soldiers on both sides of the American Revolution. In fact, the Continental Army used Franklin's lead gutters—confiscated, melted down, and turned into bullets—against the redcoats. But by then Franklin was back across the Atlantic. Congress had voted to send him away again, this time to France to negotiate an alliance with that longtime enemy of England. He departed in October 1776, accompanied by two grandsons, William Temple Franklin—the illegitimate son of his illegitimate son—and Benjamin Franklin Bache, Sally's son. This time he would be gone for nine years.

Carolinn Skyler as Marianne Kirchgaessner plays the armonica

In France, Franklin was like a modern-day celebrity, with his image adorning everything from pitchers to plates. His face, he told his sister, was "almost as well known as that of the Moon." He wore a fur cap to protect his sensitive scalp, but he continued to wear it when he realized the French considered the cap to be a symbol of his American authenticity. If that was the image they wanted, that was the image he would give them. The French people embraced this rustic American philosopher, sometimes literally. Franklin engaged in flirtatious relationships with several ladies who lived near his home in the Paris suburb of Passy. His negotiations with the French government, however, proceeded slowly. Not until the Americans defeated Gen. John Burgoyne's British army at Saratoga in October 1777 did France finally decide to cast its lot with the colonials.

Even with French help, the war ground on for four more years. In 1777, the British occupied Philadelphia, and Gen. Sir Charles Grey moved into Franklin's house. His aide was Capt. John André, later hanged as a spy for participating in Benedict Arnold's plot to betray West Point. The British treated Franklin's house reasonably well during the occupation — better than they treated the State House — but André took a Benjamin Wilson portrait of Franklin when the British left in 1778. In 1906, a Grey descendant returned the portrait, which is now in the White House.

In 1781, with French assistance, Washington defeated Gen. Charles Cornwallis at Yorktown. For all intents and purposes, the war was over. Now Franklin was thrust into the middle of peace negotiations. In September 1783, Franklin, John Adams, and John Jay signed a treaty officially ending the war with England.

In Philadelphia, Charles Willson Peale took charge of a peace celebration. He commissioned a huge victory arch that stretched across Market Street near the State House. Festooned with paintings, symbols, inscriptions, columns, garlands, statues, and busts, the fifty-seven-foot-wide structure had triple arches forty feet high and fifteen hundred lamps to illuminate it. Peale arranged a huge fireworks exhibition with seven hundred rockets to climax the whole celebration, but things went horribly awry when a rocket set the arch on fire. One man was killed in the resulting conflagration and many others injured, including Peale, who had to leap to safety from his arch.

Franklin, whose firefighting soul would have been appalled by the whole affair, was still across the Atlantic. He did not leave for the new United States of America until July 1785. Following a short and unemotional meeting with his estranged son in England, Franklin made his final journey across the Atlantic, reaching Philadelphia's Market Street Wharf on September 14. More than sixty years earlier, he had come ashore at the same

spot unnoticed, an obscure and somewhat ridiculous figure. This time, thousands of people awaited to celebrate his arrival and conduct him home to the sound of ringing bells and booming cannons.

Franklin was now near eighty and struggling with ill health. No doubt he would have enjoyed some peace and quiet. Instead, he was elected president (governor) of Pennsylvania and served three one-year terms. In 1787, he returned again to the State House as a delegate to the Constitutional Convention.

Ralph Archbold as Franklin

A visiting New England clergyman, the Reverend Manasseh Cutler, visited Franklin Court in July 1787 and wrote a delightful account of his impressions. Cutler expected to find a man "with the air of grandeur and majesty about him." Instead, he discovered "a short, fat, trunched old man, in a plain Quaker dress, bald pate, and short white locks" sitting beneath a mulberry tree. "He rose from his chair, took me by the hand, expressed his joy to see me, welcomed me to the city, and begged me to seat myself close to him. His voice was low but his countenance was open, frank, and pleasing." Cutler, Franklin, and several members of the Constitutional Convention talked outdoors until dusk. "The tea-table was spread under the tree, and Mrs. Bache, a very gross and rather homely lady, who is the only daughter of the Doctor and lives with him, served it out to the company. She had three of her children about her, over whom she appeared to have no kind of command, but who appeared to be excessively fond of their Grandpapa."

Franklin showed Cutler a two-headed snake someone had given him and was about to use it as a metaphor for an occurrence at the convention when one of the guests reminded him that all deliberations were to be kept secret. "The Doctor seemed extremely fond, through the course of the visit, of dwelling on Philosophical subjects, and particularly that of natural History," Cutler wrote. "I was highly delighted with the extensive knowledge he appeared to have of every subject, the brightness of his memory, and clearness and vivacity of all his mental faculties. Notwithstanding his age (eighty-four [he was really eighty-one]), his manners are perfectly easy, and every thing about him seemed to diffuse an unrestrained freedom and happiness. He had an incessant vein of humor, accompanied by an uncommon vivacity, which seemed as natural and involuntary as his breathing."

Walk through the archway leading from Market Street into Franklin Court today, and you might find a facsimile of the man Cutler encountered. Ralph Archbold, Philadelphia's official Ben Franklin, spends several hours a day in Franklin Court, answering questions and entertaining visitors. He has been performing as Franklin for more than thirty years. "I've been the leading

Franklin probably since Howard Da Silva passed away, in any way you want to measure it, number of performances, variety of audiences I reach, any way you want to measure it," Archbold says proudly. "There's really no one even close."

If that sounds like vanity, it's perfectly in character. "Most people dislike Vanity in others whatever Share they have of it themselves, but I give it fair Quarter wherever I meet with it, being persuaded that it is often productive of Good to the Possessor and to others that are within his Sphere of Action," Franklin wrote.

For many people Archbold *is* Ben Franklin. He appears in Philadelphia's tourism ads, provided Franklin's voice for the Lights of Liberty tour, played Franklin in the Discovery Channel's hunt for *The Greatest American* (Franklin came in fifth), speaks at hundreds of events a year, and answers questions as a spectral presence in "Franklin's Ghost" in the Lights of Liberty lobby.

On a typical day, you can find Archbold sitting on a bench in Franklin Court beneath a drawing of the scene Cutler described in 1787. Crowds of schoolchildren gather around him and ask questions. So do adults. "There are some misconceptions," Archbold says. "They think that he had three hundred illegitimate children or something like that. Women come up to me and say, 'You were a womanizer,' and I say, 'You'll have to define that term for me, madam.' 'It means you like women.' 'Well, then, that's true.' 'It means women like you.' 'Well, that's true. I would hope so. So is there something wrong with this?' They'll chide me about leaving my wife in America. I'll talk about how she wouldn't get on board a ship. As evidenced by some of my friends, I encouraged her to come over. She wouldn't come over. That was her choice as much as my choice."

In general, though, people connect with Franklin. Whether it's his humor, his kite, or his surface appearance of jolly benevolence, people like him. "Franklin is more approachable than most of the other figures in our history," Archbold says. "I have walked down the street with someone playing Washington, someone playing Lincoln, and they'll approach Franklin. The other two don't feel as approachable. So Franklin is like a friend.

Franklin Court
(800) 537-7676

The Chestnut Street entrance to Franklin Court is across the street from Carpenters' Hall. Be sure to give yourself enough time to visit the underground museum, the Printing Shop, and the Fragments of Franklin Court exhibit. You can also get a B. Free Franklin cancellation at the post office. (Franklin was a postmaster himself.) Between 10 A.M. and 12 noon on weekdays during the peak tourist season, Franklin impersonator Ralph Archbold sits outside the museum and answers questions. Dean Bennett appears as Franklin in the film screened in the underground museum's theater. Franklin Court is operated by the National Park Service as part of Independence National Historical Park. The Underground Museum is open from 9 A.M. to 5 P.M. daily; the Printing Office from 10 A.M. to 5 P.M.; and Fragments of Franklin Court from 9 A.M. to 11 A.M. The hours can vary seasonally, so check things out at the Visitor Center first.

And probably that's because of his sense of humor, the maxims that he had. We feel we've heard them since we were young, and we've identified with them, and we like Franklin."

People go to Franklin Court to find traces of the real Ben Franklin, but the sad thing is that they will find only traces. Franklin's relatives tore his house down in 1812 so they could subdivide the property. Years later, the city put a road right through the site. The National Park Service obtained the land in 1954 and began archeological excavations that uncovered portions of the foundation, the kitchen's brick floor, privy pits, and various artifacts. You can peer into covered excavations and see some of the objects the archeologists uncovered, but you can't visit Franklin's home.

There aren't even any contemporary drawings to show us what it looked like. We know it was made of brick, was thirty-four feet on each side, and had three stories with three rooms on each floor. In 1787, Franklin completed an extension that gave him half again more room, something he needed to keep from being crowded by his daughter and her family. On the second floor of the new portion, he installed a library with more than four thousand volumes, the largest private library in North America. According to Cutler, "The walls were covered with book-shelves filled with books; besides, there are four large alcoves, extending two-thirds of the length of the Chamber, filled in the same manner." To reach books on the higher shelves, Franklin invented a long gripping device, now on display in the Franklin Court museum. "Over his mantel-tree, he has a prodigious number of medals, busts, and casts in wax or plaster of Paris, which are the effigies of the most noted characters in Europe," Cutler noted.

After Franklin died, his magnificent library was broken up and dispersed. In the 1950s, the Library Company's Edwin Wolf commenced a remarkable bit of detective work and tracked down roughly one-quarter of the books, identifying them from the markings written inside to show their proper places on Franklin's bookshelves.

The house is gone, but the Park Service commissioned Philadelphia architect Robert Venturi to create its spectral presence with a stainless steel outline of the building. Next to it, another steel frame shows the location of the print house Franklin built for grandson Benjamin Franklin Bache. Bache later published a newspaper called the *Aurora* from 322 Market Street, where the National Park Service has a re-creation of his office. Bache attacked the administration of John Adams with such vigor that he was arrested under the Alien and Sedition Laws. He died in 1798 of yellow fever while preparing his defense, and his wife took over the newspaper—and the attacks on Adams.

Number 322 Market Street was one of the buildings Franklin constructed to use as rental properties. First he tore down two structures with which he had personal connections. One of them was John Read's house, where Deborah first saw young Franklin more than six decades earlier, and where Franklin lodged when

Outline of Franklin's house (rear) and his grandson's print house by Robert Venturi

he arrived in Philadelphia. The other was once Samuel Keimer's print shop.

Franklin built two new buildings, numbers 316 and 318, around an arch that allowed access to his house back in the court. The buildings stand today on Market Street, their fronts reconstructed to present their appearance from Franklin's time. Number 318 houses an exhibit called "Fragments of Franklin Court." The building's interior has been gutted. Inside, a stairway with platforms allows you to examine the walls and see the ghostly traces of joists and fireplaces and closets. There are cases throughout with artifacts archeologists discovered: oyster shells, bowls, pitchers, chamber pots, ivory implements, the detritus of everyday life in the eighteenth century. Museum artifacts now, back then they were hardly worth the effort it took to toss them into the privy.

Below Franklin Court is an underground museum that was probably considered pretty hot stuff when it opened in 1975, but it seems a little dated today. There are a few relics—Franklin's desk, his book gripper, reproductions of family portraits—but

320 and 322 Market Street

the centerpiece is "Franklin on the World Stage," a sunken arena with detailed little wooden figures. A platform in the middle descends and then rises, with different figures on it to represent Franklin arguing against the Stamp Act at the House of Commons in 1766, at Versailles in 1778, and at the Constitutional Convention in 1787. Recorded dialogue explains what Franklin did at those long-ago events.

The museum's other highlight is the Franklin Exchange, with ranks of beige telephones on individual stands. At first glance, it appears to be a surrealistic art project, something by Man Ray or Andy Warhol. Visitors can use the phones to dial numbers listed on the opposite wall and hear historical figures talk about Franklin. I dial up John Adams and hear that dyspeptic New Englander's measured appraisal, then listen to Thomas Jefferson remark: "I served with General Washington in the legislature of Virginia before the Revolution, and during it with Dr. Franklin in Congress. I never heard either of them speak ten minutes at a time, nor to any but the main point which was to decide the question."

Franklin remained in character and spoke little as a delegate at the Constitutional Convention, held from May to September 1787 at the State House, now shorn of its rotten steeple. He was so ill that he had to be carried to the meetings in a sedan chair by four prisoners from the nearby jail, yet he attended every day for four months. When I visit the Assembly Room and gaze around the august chamber, with its battleship gray walls, high ceilings, and tables covered with green baize, I experience it in air-conditioned comfort. The delegates in 1787 had created their revolutionary document during a hot, humid, fly-infested Philadelphia summer. After waiting in line to go through the tight, post-9/11 security, I am somewhat reassured to learn that such concerns aren't totally new. When Manasseh Cutler toured the State House during the Convention in 1787, he noted sentries posted in front of the closed doors of the Assembly Room as the debate went on inside. They appeared "to be very alert in the performance of their duty," he reported.

National Constitution Center

525 Arch Street ★ (215) 409-6600
www.constitutioncenter.org

In the twilight of his life, Franklin served as a delegate to the Constitutional Convention, and you can find him today among the forty-two lifesize statues of the thirty-nine men who signed the Constitution and the three who decided not to in the National Constitution Center's Signers Hall. Opened in 2003, the center offers the latest in interactive technology to make the U.S. Constitution come to life for young and old alike. The visit begins in the Kimmel Theater, with an introduction that combines a live actor with light and sound effects. In the 67,785-square-foot exhibit space, kids enjoy being sworn in as president, with the ceremony visible on a large TV screen above them. You can also vote for your favorite president, sit at the Supreme Court bench, or learn about the U.S. government through computer kiosks. The Llewellyn Citizens' Café, just outside Signer's Hall, offers beautiful views of Independence Hall through huge windows. The National Constitution Center is open daily, except for Thanksgiving and Christmas, Sunday through Friday from 9:30 A.M. to 5 P.M., Saturday from 9:30 A.M. to 6 P.M. Admission is $9 for adults and $7 for children, students, and seniors.

One of the only original pieces of furniture in Independence Hall today is the chair that John Hancock used in 1776 and George Washington in 1787 as the Constitutional Convention's president. The chair's back bore the carving of a sun. "I have often in the course of the session, and the vicissitudes of my hopes and fears to its issue, looked at that behind the President without being able to tell whether it was rising or setting," Franklin observed at the convention's end. "But now at length I have the happiness to know that it is a rising and not a setting sun." The signers of the Constitution, Franklin among them, once again used the Philip Syng inkwell.

Franklin himself was now a setting sun, but he took up one last role before he died, as president of the Pennsylvania Society for Promoting the Abolition of Slavery and the Relief of Negroes Unlawfully Held in Bondage. His conversion to the cause had come somewhat late. He had owned slaves for thirty years, and he and William had taken two with them to England. Franklin was an eighteenth-century man, with all that century's prejudices. In 1751, he wrote a paper advocating the exclusion of non-whites from America. "But perhaps I am partial to the Complexion of my Country, for such Kind of Partiality is natural to Mankind," he concluded. His views evolved, however. He helped organize schools for black children and developed "a higher Opinion of the Natural Capacities of the black Race than I have ever before entertained." In 1790, he published a satire intended to expose the follies of slaveholders, written in the voice of Sidi Mehemet

The African American Museum in Philadelphia

701 Arch St. ★ (215) 574-0380

www.aampmuseum.org

One of the last public roles Franklin took on was president of the Pennsylvania Society for Promoting the Abolition of Slavery. The Abolitionist moment later adopted the Liberty Bell as its symbol, and Philadelphia became an important center for Underground Railroad activity. The African American Museum in Philadelphia, which opened in 1976 on the corner of Arch Street and Seventh Street, offers a celebration of the city's African American art and culture, with a number of permanent and temporary exhibits. The museum is open Tuesday through Saturday from 10 A.M. to 5 P.M. and Sunday from 12 noon to 5 P.M. Admission is $8 for adults and $6 for children, seniors, and students.

Ibrahim of Algiers, who defended the practice of enslaving Christians.

It was Franklin's last piece of public writing. He died on the night of April 17, 1790, in his home in Franklin Court. About twenty thousand people turned out for his funeral when he was laid to rest next to his wife at Christ Church Burial Ground.

Christ Church had purchased this land for its dead in 1719. The oldest known stone dates from 1723; Deborah Read's father arrived here a year later. The older stones were made from a soft Pennsylvania marble, and over the centuries, acid rain has obliterated the inscriptions. Many of the markers people had erected so that they would be remembered forever have been wiped clean, as though erased by the hand of God. Fortunately for posterity, in 1864 a church warden noted the damage and copied out all the inscriptions he could still read. Some survived because the ground swallowed up the stones and protected them from the pollution, but many slipped away from both sight and memory. Among the missing are those of Joseph Hewes and George Ross, two signers of the Declaration of Independence. Though they have plaques,

Christ Church Burial Ground
Arch St. and Fifth St. ★ www.oldchristchurch.org

The Franklins are buried in Christ Church Burial Ground, at the corner of Arch Street and Fifth Street. You can see their graves through the fence on Arch Street, but it's worth the small admission fee to wander around this historic graveyard and find some of Franklin's acquaintances. Charts are available near the entrance and prove very helpful, as many of the inscriptions have weathered into illegibility. It's a good idea to take a guided tour; the guides provide plenty of interesting background. Toss a penny on Franklin's grave for good luck. The Burial Ground is open Monday through Saturday, 10 A.M. to 4 P.M. and Sunday from noon to 4 P.M., weather permitting. Cost is $2 for adults and $1 for students.

no one knows exactly where their bodies lie. By 1976, time had taken such a toll on the burial ground that Christ Church closed it to the public. It reopened in 2003 after a $500,000 restoration.

As he did in life, Franklin has many connections here. Thomas Bond is buried nearby. So is David Hall, Franklin's longtime printing partner. Philip Syng, who died in 1789, is buried here with his wife and their fourteen children. His gravesite had been lost for years, until one of his descendants, J. Del Conner of the Philadelphia Society for the Preservation of Landmarks, discovered it by accident in 2003. Samuel and Elizabeth Powel, whose hospitality Franklin had enjoyed, are buried side by side not far from Franklin's grave. Powel, one of Franklin's pallbearers, died three years later of yellow fever. Thomas Truxton, who had commanded the London packet that brought Franklin home from Europe in 1785, lies at the burial ground's other end. Another signer of the Declaration of Independence, Francis Hopkinson, was a writer, composer, and member of the Library Company and the American Philosophical Society. Franklin willed his scientific instruments to Hopkinson; now the two signers share this little bit of real estate.

Franklin lies in the corner next to an open fence along Arch Street. Visitors like to toss pennies on his grave, which supposedly brings good luck. No one knows the tradition's origin, but it may derive from "a penny saved is a penny earned," an adage commonly attributed to Poor Richard. Each year, Christ Church earns about $500 in change from Poor Richard's grave.

Deborah lies next to him, near their young son Francis, who died of smallpox in 1736 at age four. As late as 1772, Franklin still grieved, writing his sister about "my son Franky, though now dead thirty-six years, whom I have seldom since seen equalled in everything, and whom to this day I cannot think of without a sigh." Sally Franklin and her husband, Richard Bache, are nearby too.

The gray stone slab that covers Franklin's grave bears a simple inscription, "Benjamin and Deborah Franklin," and it's dated 1790. (Deborah's death date apparently was not worth mentioning.) This is the inscription Franklin requested in his will, when he was old and tired and ready for death. Back when he was the

Visitors toss pennies on Franklin's grave

ambitious young man who formed the Junto and enjoyed convivial evenings with appropriate pauses for wine, he had written a humorous epigraph that better captures the wit and personality of the Benjamin Franklin we like to remember:

The Body of B. Franklin/Printer,
Like the Cover of an old Book,
Its Contents torn out,
And stript of its Lettering and Gilding,
Lies here, Food for Worms.
But the Work shall not be wholly lost.
For it will, as he believ'd, appear once more,
In a new & more perfect Edition,
Corrected and amended
By the Author.

FOLLOWING FRANKLIN

Walking Tour and Maps

★

1 **Penn's Landing** on the Delaware River waterfront is the perfect spot to start a walking tour of Franklin's Philadelphia. Young Ben arrived here in 1723.

2 A plaque on the stairwell in the **subway station** at Market Street and Second Street marks the spot where Franklin established his first print shop.

3 Just across the street is **Church Street**, once known as Pewter Platter Alley. The entrance to the Junto's headquarters in Robert Grace's house was from this narrow lane.

4 **Christ Church** is just up Second Street from Market. Its steeple has been a Philadelphia landmark since 1754.

5 **Elfreth's Alley** is farther up Second Street.

6 The **Fireman's Hall Museum** is in a former firehouse on Second Street beyond Elfreth's Alley.

7 Retrace your steps down Second Street and turn the corner onto Arch Street to find the **Betsy Ross House**, one of the city's most popular attractions. Whether Betsy Ross created the first American flag here remains doubtful, but there's no doubt the story has endured as part of the nation's mythology. (215) 686-1252; www.betsyrosshouse.org.

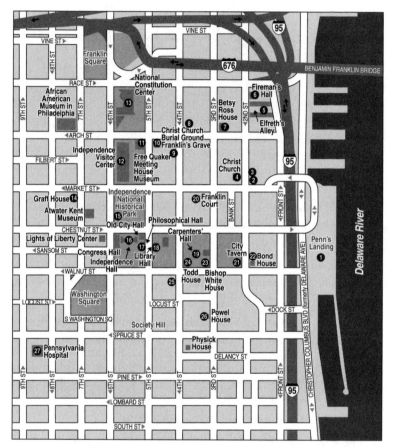

*Numbers on the map refer to
the Walking Tour stops.*

8 According to local tradition, Franklin performed his famous kite experiment on the site of **Loxley Court**, off Arch Street.

9 From the other side of Arch Street, head down Fourth Street past the Holiday Inn to find the marker noting the location of the **New Building** Franklin helped establish "for the use of any preacher of any religious persuasion who might desire to say something to the people at Philadelphia," and which later housed the academy Franklin founded.

10 **Christ Church Burial Ground** is at the corner of Arch Street and Fifth Street.

11 Across Arch Street from the Burial Ground is the **Free Quaker Meeting House**, established by breakaway Friends who supported taking arms against the British during the American Revolution.

12 The **Independence Visitor Center**, at the corner of Sixth Street and Market Street, is the best place to organize your stay in Philadelphia.

13 The **National Constitution Center** is also nearby.

14 Thomas Jefferson wrote the Declaration of Independence in his rented rooms at the **Graff House**. The National Park Service operates a re-creation of the building.

15 Pass through the **Liberty Bell Center** to reach Independence Hall.

16 **Independence Hall** tours include a brief orientation and stops in the Assembly Room and Court Room. Tickets are not required to visit the "Great Essentials" exhibit, Old City Hall, or Congress Hall.

17 **Philosophical Hall**, on Fifth Street, is the headquarters of the American Philosophical Society and houses its small museum.

18 Facing Philosophical Hall from across Fifth Street is the facade of the American Philosophical Society, which re-creates the looks of **Library Hall**.

19 **Carpenters' Hall** was the meeting place of the First Continental Congress.

20 The Market Street entrance to **Franklin Court** is across the street from Carpenters' Hall.

21 By now you've probably worked up an appetite. Fortunately, you're not far from **City Tavern**, the re-creation of "the most genteel tavern in America."

22 Just across Second Street from the tavern is the **Thomas Bond House**, once the home of Franklin's friend Dr. Thomas Bond, who approached Franklin with the idea of starting a hospital. Now it's a bed-and-breakfast.

23 The **Bishop White House** was home to the onetime rector of Christ Church.

24 The **Todd House** is where the future Dolley Madison once lived.

25 It's worth a slight detour down Fourth Street to visit the headquarters of the **Philadelphia Contributorship**, the insurance company that Franklin founded in 1752.

26 The **Powel House** is farther down Third Street.

27 To reach the **Pennsylvania Hospital**, continue down Third Street and turn right onto Spruce Street. Enjoy the elegant brick Federal-style buildings of Society Hill as you make your way down to Eighth Street and the hospital. The entrance on Eighth Street will take you to the Welcome Desk.

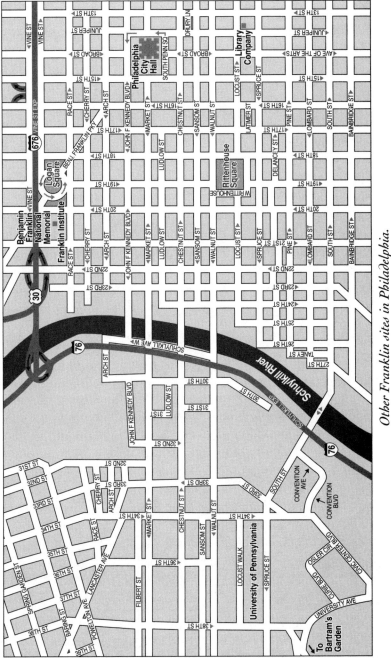

Other Franklin sites in Philadelphia.

FRANKLIN IN PHILADELPHIA
A Limited Chronology
★

1706 Born in Boston, January 6 (changed to January 17 when calendar was adjusted in 1752).

1723 Arrives in Philadelphia and begins working for Samuel Keimer, printer.

1724 Sails to London, November 5.

1726 Returns to Philadelphia, October 11.

1727 Forms Junto.

1728 Begins a printing business with Hugh Meredith.

1729 Starts publishing *The Pennsylvania Gazette*.

1730 Begins living with Deborah Read, September 1.

1731 Forms the Library Company of Philadelphia. William Franklin born?

1732 Publishes the first edition of *Poor Richard's Almanac*. Son Francis born, October 20.

1736 Becomes clerk of the Pennsylvania Assembly. Founds the Union Fire Company. Francis dies of smallpox, November 21.

1737 Appointed Philadelphia's postmaster.

1743 Founds the American Philosophical Society. Meets Archibald Spencer in Boston and becomes interested in electricity. Daughter Sarah born, August 31.

1748 Begins printing partnership with David Hall and retires. Elected to Philadelphia's Common Council.

1749 Becomes president of the trustees of the Academy of Philadelphia.

1751 Helps found the Pennsylvania Hospital. Elected to the Pennsylvania Assembly and becomes an alderman for Philadelphia.

1752 Helps found the Philadelphia Contributorship. Performs kite experiment.

1753 Becomes postmaster for North America, a position he shares with William Hunter.

1755 Helps supply Gen. William Braddock.

1756 Becomes a colonel in the Pennsylvania militia.

1757 Sails for London, June 20.

1762 Returns to Philadelphia, November 1.

1763 Begins work on his house in Franklin Court.

1764 Elected speaker of the Pennsylvania Assembly, May 26. Defeated in election, October 1. Sails to England, November 9.

1774 Deborah Franklin dies, December 19.

1775 Returns to Philadelphia, May 5. Chosen as a delegate to the Second Continental Congress the next day.

1776 Declaration of Independence adopted, July 4. Sails for France, October 26.

1785 Returns to Philadelphia, September 14. Elected president (essentially governor) of Pennsylvania.

1786 Builds an extension to his house.

1787 Elected president of the Pennsylvania Society for Promoting the Abolition of Slavery. Becomes a delegate to the Constitutional Convention.

1790 Dies at age eighty-four, April 17.

Further Reading and Information

★

BOOKS

Brands, H. W. *The First American: The Life and Times of Benjamin Franklin*. New York: Doubleday, 2000.

Bridenbaugh, Carl, and Jessica Bridenbaugh. *Rebels and Gentlemen: Philadelphia in the Age of Franklin*. New York: Oxford University Press, 1942.

Cotter, John L., Daniel G. Roberts, and Michael Parrington. *The Buried Past: An Archeological History of Philadelphia*. Philadelphia: University of Pennsylvania, 1992.

Cutler, William Parker, and Julia Perkins Cutler. *Life, Journals and Correspondence of Rev. Manasseh Cutler, LLD*. Cincinnati: R. Clarke and Co., 1888.

Elfreth's Alley Association. *Inside These Doors: A Historic Guidebook of the Homes of Elfreth's Alley, a National Historic Landmark*. Philadelphia: Elfreth's Alley Association, 2004.

Fleming, Thomas, ed. *Benjamin Franklin: A Biography in His Own Words*. New York: Harper & Row, 1972.

Franklin, Benjamin. *Writings*. New York: Library of America, 1987. Contents: Boston and London, 1722–1726; Philadelphia, 1726–1757; London, 1757–1775; Paris, 1776–1785; Philadelphia, 1785–1790; Poor Richard's Almanac, 1733–1758; The Autobiography.

Gough, Deborah Mathias. *Christ Church, Philadelphia: The Nation's Church in a Changing City*. Philadelphia: University of Philadelphia Press, 1995.

Green, James. *Poor Richard's Books: An Exhibition of Books Owned by Benjamin Franklin Now on the Shelves of the Library Company of Philadelphia*. Philadelphia: Library Company of Philadelphia, 1990.

Isaacson, Walter. *Benjamin Franklin: An American Life*. New York: Simon & Schuster, 2003.

Kashatus, William C., III. *Historic Philadelphia: The City, Symbols and Patriots, 1681–1800*. Lanham, MD: University Press of America, 1992.

Kelley, Joseph H. *Life and Times in Colonial Philadelphia*. Harrisburg, PA: Stackpole Books, 1973.

Labaree, Leonard W., Ralph L. Ketcham, Helen C. Boatfield, and Helene H. Fineman, eds. *The Autobiography of Benjamin Franklin.* New Haven, CT: Yale University Press, 1964.

Library Company of Philadelphia. *"At the Instance of Benjamin Franklin": A Brief History of the Library Company of Philadelphia.* Philadelphia: Library Company of Philadelphia, 1995.

Lopez, Claude-Anne. *Benjamin Franklin's "Good House": The Story of Franklin Court.* Washington, DC: National Park Service, 1981.

———. *My Life with Benjamin Franklin.* New Haven, CT: Yale University Press, 2000.

Mires, Charlene. *Independence Hall in American Memory.* Philadelphia: University of Pennsylvania Press, 2002.

Morgan, Edmund S. *Benjamin Franklin.* New Haven, CT: Yale University Press, 2003.

Moss, Roger W. *Historic Houses of Philadelphia.* Photographs by Tom Crane. Philadelphia: University of Pennsylvania Press, 1998.

———. *Historic Sacred Places of Philadelphia.* Photographs by Tom Crane. Philadelphia: University of Pennsylvania Press, 2005.

Philadelphia Contributorship. *The Philadelphia Contributorship 250th Anniversary.* Philadelphia: Philadelphia Contributorship for the Insurance of Houses from Loss by Fire, 2002.

Schiffer, Michael Brian. *Draw the Lightning Down: Benjamin Franklin and Electrical Technology in the Age of Enlightenment.* Los Angeles: University of California Press, 2003.

Talbott, Page, ed. *Benjamin Franklin: In Search of a Better World.* New Haven, CT: Yale University Press, 2005.

Tucker, Tom. *Bolt of Fate: Benjamin Franklin and His Electric Kite Hoax.* New York: Public Affairs, 2003.

Van Doren, Carl. *Benjamin Franklin.* New York: Viking Press, 1938.

ON THE WEB

www.benfranklin2006.org
The Friends of Franklin is a society of Franklin admirers that offers occasional events and tours.

www.ushistory.org/phnc
Philadelphia's Historic Neighborhood Consortium is a confederation of more than forty attractions. Includes links to member websites.

www.gophila.com
The Greater Philadelphia Tourism Marketing Corporation website provides a great beginning for planning a visit to Philadelphia.

www.pcvb.org
The Philadelphia Convention and Visitors Bureau

Index

★

The Tercentenary

★

The year 2006 marks the three hundredth anniversary of Franklin's birth, and Philadelphia plans to celebrate in style. The tercentenary's centerpiece will be "Benjamin Franklin: In Search of a Better World," a traveling exhibition that will remain at the National Constitution Center until April 30, 2006. It includes 250 Franklin artifacts gathered from private and public collections, as well as interactive displays and videos to bring Franklin's life, times, and personality to life.

In January, the Franklin Institute will debut "Ben's Electrical Spectacular," an interactive experience that will examine Franklin's work with electricity. The American Philosophical Society will have an exhibit, "The Princess and the Patriot: Ekaterina Dashkova, Benjamin Franklin and the Age of Enlightenment," from February 17 until December 31, 2006. The Library Company of Philadelphia opens "Franklin and the Book," an exhibit highlighting Franklin's life as a writer, publisher, and printer. It will run from May to December. The Philadelphia Museum of Art will put the spotlight on a Frenchman's iconic bust of Franklin for "In Pursuit of Genius: Jean-Antoine Houdon and the Sculpted Portraits of Benjamin Franklin," from May 13 to July 30.

Throughout 2006, these institutions and others will also sponsor lectures, conferences, and online exhibitions about Franklin and his times. To learn more about the Tercentenary events, visit the official website at www.benfranklin300.org.